THE TERRIBLE BABY NAME BOOK

THE TERRIBLE BABY NAME BOOK

JOHN ZINSSER
JACK ZINSSER

ULYSSES PRESS

Published in 2026 by
ULYSSES PRESS
an imprint of The Stable Book Group
32 Court Street, Suite 2109
Brooklyn, NY 11201
www.ulyssespress.com

Library of Congress Control Number: 2026941290
ISBN: 978-1-64604-956-1
eISBN: 978-1-64604-957-8

Acquisitions editor: Brian McLendon
Managing editor: Claire Chun
Copy editor: Caroline Ernst
Proofreader: Renee Rutledge
Cover design: Jack Zinsser
Interior design: Abbey Gregory
Illustrations: Charlotte Zinsser

Printed in China
10 9 8 7 6 5 4 3 2 1

Dedicated to Papas the cat

Introduction

Dear Beloved Parent-to-Be,

You are about to embark on one of the most significant tasks of your life: the naming of your precious new baby.

This is a most tender and special opportunity, often worked on in tandem with a partner or spouse. The name you bestow upon your newborn will mold them over the course of the rest of their life. Your choice will give your child his/her/their special character: In a sense, they 'become' the name itself. It signifies identity in its truest form.

Sigmund Freud has given us our modern concept of ego (which he called 'the I'). One's ego defines one's intellectual and social self. Ego is constantly present and on display during daily interactions. Your child's development of ego begins with their recognition of their own name. In turn, others come to recognize their name as a representation of their personality. Freud's follower, French psychologist Jacques Lacan, expanded on the essentialness of this phenomenon. He writes: 'The signifier represents a subject for another signifier'. Simply put, the name you select for your child will ultimately help to shape their station, and even their larger destiny, in the world.

The chain of life will soon continue. Your chosen name will be officially pronounced first at the baptism or bris, or any other rite of passage along their journey toward adulthood. It will certainly appear on the kindergarten class roster, read aloud by the teacher on the first day of school. Birthday parties, Bar Mitzvahs and Bat Mitzvahs, and other personal celebrations will prominently, feature the name foremost.

The name you select will be further reinforced at the issuing of the first driver's license, passport, or a draft notice. Triumphantly, the name of your progeny will one day be boldly announced over the PA system at high school and college graduation ceremonies.

Importantly, in addition, you must be aware that—finally and sadly—your chosen name will one day be etched upon a tombstone, forever cherished and remembered, and potentially passed along to future generations.

Traditionally, religion has played a central role in this portentous undertaking, expressing a larger sense of spiritual devotion and belonging. Yet, originality still remains key. In this case, imagine the thrill if you had been the first parent to name your child 'Jesus' or 'Muhammad' or 'Siddhartha'. Of course, ordinary Biblical names such as 'John', 'Seth', or 'Rebecca' remain steadfastly popular—and still prove sturdy and dependable. Trending Biblical names currently include: 'Asher', 'Zoe', and 'Silas'. We suggest you go even further. What about 'Nebuchadnezzar'?) Or 'Mahershalalhashbaz', or even 'Zaphnathpaaneah'? Try coming to your Bible studies class with one of those!

It will come as no surprise that our lives are deeply affected by the celebrities and influencers who demand our constant and unwaning attention. Likewise, we are riveted to the private family lives of our politicians and titans of industry. These figures have turned to the naming process as an opportunity to assert their own family's larger presence as a 'brand'.

Just look at the offspring of our recently elected presidents of the United States. The name 'Hunter Biden' appears to have anticipated keen predatory instincts and well-documented lifelong dalliances with danger. 'Tiffany Trump' honors an American luxury jewelry brand whose flagship store stands directly next door to Trump Tower on New York City's Fifth Avenue. 'Barron Trump' has literally grown in physical stature to meet the noble expectations of his name. Perhaps 'Chelsea Clinton' first led the way, with a name that has now become synonymous with chic contemporary New York art galleries.

Gwyneth Paltrow, leading style maven and founder of the lifestyle brand Goop, broke new aesthetic ground by naming one of her children 'Moses' and the other 'Apple'. Today, we routinely find such names as 'Onion' and 'Shallot' to be not only charming, but also savory and sweet.

By now, we know that nature and its physical glories can serve as wonderful inspiration. Think of the late actor 'River' Phoenix or his sister 'Rain' Phoenix. Both were gifted these names by their own free-spirited hippie parents (who, it is known, were itinerant fruit pickers and served as missionaries for the Children of God cult in South America). If only they had been bold enough to call one of their little ones 'Puddle'!

More recently, the rap artist Kanye West (who had already renamed himself 'Ye') joined with his wife at the time, fashion entrepreneur Kim Kardashian, to name their daughter 'North' West. One cannot help but wonder if they were paying tribute to the majestic beauty of the northwestern US states of Oregon and Washington?

Tesla mogul Elon Musk has riveted our attention not just with his technical wizardry and financial savvy, but also with his leadership in redefining what a 'family unit' can be. To date, he is known to have sired some 14 children with four different women. He starts, it seems, by choosing partners with beguiling names. Three of these offspring are with ex-girlfriend, the Canadian singer Grimes. And another four are with Neuralink executive Shivon Zilis. Many of the copious litter have simply catchy names such as 'Kai', 'Saxon', and 'Damian'. But more recently, Musk has once again captured national attention by naming one son 'Techno Mechanicus', another 'X AE A-XII', and a daughter 'Exa Dark Sideræl'. To answer any criticism, Musk has simply tweeted: 'Doing my best to help the underpopulation crisis'.

Meantime, the celebrity children's name roster keeps growing unabated: 'Blue Ivy', 'Bronx', 'Audio', 'Cricket', 'Brother', 'Denim', 'Dream', 'Pilot Inspektor', 'Everest', 'Maple', 'Moroccan', 'Puma', 'Riot', 'Saga Blade', and 'Zolten' are just a few of many.

Know, also, that a time may come when your offspring may choose to rename themselves. This is a cathartic process of 're-baptization' (as we psychologists term it), 'replacing' oneself into a new self-selected rubric. Such was certainly the case when rapper and impresario Sean John Combs renamed himself first 'Puff Daddy', and then, simply, 'P. Diddy'. He retained the 'Sean John' moniker his parents had first lovingly bestowed upon him to launch his multimillion-dollar clothing line. It may be noted that the recent federal case mounted against him was simply called 'United States of America v. Sean Combs'. The indictment listed 'Victim-1', 'Victim-2', and 'Jane', names that themselves signify anonymity, but also, we suggest, now carry a certain understated charm of their own.

Scholars in the naming field have taught us that the practice of renaming may arise from a desire for greater autonomy, or new gender identity, or simply assertion of personality. It is also a clinically proven coping mechanism for trauma. In extreme cases, it may even be the result of psychosis. Typical reappointed names have included: 'Austin', 'Gwen', 'Neo', 'Silvia Lucia', and 'Violet

Woods'. In African American culture, such self-naming is considered an instrument of empowerment.

One may heighten this aura of importance by insisting on referring to oneself in the third person. This practice is called illeism. In linguistic terms, this creates emotional distance and allows for better decision-making. It can also project a powerful or narcissistic persona. Lebron James stating: 'Lebron James has to do what makes LeBron James happy'.

What about the delicate matter of adopting a baby? If, perhaps, the child is older than an infant, coming with a preexisting name from an exotic land such as Mainland China, Siberia, or the Galapagos Islands, please don't hesitate to rename him or her or them, so that they may be better able to assimilate with their new American peers. May we go further, and suggest that you name your new foreign interloper after one of our own great American metropolises—such as Minneapolis or San Antonio—to better assert a new national identity?

Alternatively, you could also find yourself welcoming a stepchild to your family, in which case a change of name could serve as an opportunity to perform a refreshing reboot.

Importantly, we are using the opportunity of this book's publication to introduce a practice at the very vanguard of naming today: the selection and adaptation of a preexisting product name. At first, the use or employment of such names may seem downright brash, zany, or taboo. Especially if such a name must legally be accompanied by the typographically challenging © or ™ symbol. Getting past this, however, can open up liberating and exciting uncharted territory. The trend has been led by the ever-forward-thinking Swedes, who have now embraced names such as 'Miele™' and 'Saab™'. This has not only become socially acceptable but is downright vogue. In the list of names we present in this volume, we challenge you to open your sights to the richness of this very novel lexical source. Such stylish monikers as 'Subaru™', 'Lexapro™', and 'Fantastik™' await you. These are sure to not only make your child stand out as very special but also impress with already established connotations of quality and reliability.

And, lest we forget, another great contemporary resource is the acronym. As adapted to a name, these special abbreviations can carry bold panache and suggest myriad layers of meaning. An acronym employs the initial letters of a multiword phrase to form a new word, one that often packs a wallop with extreme brevity and élan. We associate such terms with the dawn of the space age and the Cold War, as they condense technical information: SONAR (Sound Navigation and Ranging), RADAR (Radio Detection and Ranging), NORAD (North American Aerospace Defense Command), and even SETI (Search for Extraterrestrial Intelligence). Today, the acronyms that we suggest on our list tell us much about ourselves and our present times: ASAP, D.A.R.E., FIFA, FLOTUS, FOMO, ICE, IMAX, LOL, MDMA, NSFW, OSHA, STEM, and, of course, YOLO, to mention only a few.

In short, we are at the dawn of a golden linguistic age. The fine art of naming your baby is now more than a simple act of parental responsibility. It will create for your new precious being an adventure that will last a lifetime—and perhaps even beyond!

In summation, as our nation's esteemed baby advisor, pediatrician Dr. Benjamin Spock, beseeched an entire generation of would-be parents: 'Trust yourself. You know more than you think'.

In short, dare to be bold in the most important life decision for your child. And enjoy the fruits of your ultimate choice.

Respectfully submitted, on the occasion of the publication of this important and groundbreaking source book,

—Dr. L. Titus Carpathian
Tenured professor of Child Psychology
and Naming Nomenclature
University of Minnesota, Minnesota City, Minnesota

To the Users of This Book: Our Personal Challenge to You

The baby names presented here, some 3,500, are listed alphabetically.

It is our hope that this will prove freeing, that you will dive in anywhere to begin your process of exploration and discovery.

We have employed extensive research in assembling this list: The myriad sources reflect today's complexly layered information age, where historical and contemporary references collide. This way, allusion and metaphor can leap forth with each reader's individual associations, memories, and larger experiences. We only admonish you, don't let your dream become a nightmare.

Your family possesses special and singular qualities, even quirks, and certainly virtues. So, how can you express these through the act of naming?

We suggest first speaking the potential name aloud. And, at the same time, adding your surname, also aloud. This way, you will immediately get a sense of the full name's proper rhythm and cadence. Its sound.

You may discover that the name already starts to resonate, to feel more natural.

In places, we have provided phonetic pronunciation guides to aid this means of innate aural discovery.

Choosing one of the names listed here will be merely the beginning of an ongoing story. This is the name that will help shape your baby's own eventual path: unique, celebrated, and perhaps even prophetic. Whether your child becomes president or ditch digger, they deserve distinction.

Let's take a moment to examine some great names from literature: Jane Eyre *(Jane Eyre)*, Atticus Finch *(To Kill a Mockingbird)*, Stephen Dedalus *(Ulysses)*, Sal Paradise *(On the Road)*. In the case of these characters, the central protagonists of great novels, we learn that we connote a name with deeper character traits.

In a Jungian sense (based on the teachings of the Swiss psychologist Carl Jung), the name itself becomes a heroic archetype, to be explored by the one who possesses it over the course of his/her/their long and richly complex life course.

So, dip in anywhere you like, and begin your adventure today.

TERRIBLE BABY NAMES LIST

A

Aardvark
Abba
Abilify
Abominable
Absinthe
Absolut
Acćent
Acid
Acquired
Actually
Adaption
Adderall
Adhesive
Adobe
Adverb
Afghanistan
Afghan Kush
African American
Afterlife
Aftershock
Agent Orange
Agony
Ahab
Ahora
Ahora Mismo
AI

AI

(AY-eye)

Before we even begin to delve into the profundity of this entry's possible naming ramifications, let's consider the possible ways 'AI' may be pronounced: 'Ay-Eye', or more directly, simply 'Eye'. Now, weigh that simple verbal declaration against the challenges the name poses. The fate of human intellect itself is at stake, subject to technological revision. The result represents a challenge: We mortals must always ultimately triumph over 'The Machine', if only through our unpredictable human nature and raw animal tenacity.

Aimless
Airport
Air-Plort
Aer Lingus
Ajax
Alas
Albatross
Aleister Crowley
Alexa Amazon Echo
Algebra
Algebra II
Alien
Alive
Alkali
Alkaline
All-Bran
Allergy
Almond
Almond Joy
Almonds
Alone
Aloof
Alpo
Alprazolam
Already
Altoid
Aluminum
Amazon Prime
Ambien
Ambition
Ambulance
Amen
American Girl
American Pie
American Spirit
American Spirit Blue
American Spirit Yellow
American Standard
Ammo
Amnesia
Amnesia
Amphetamine
Amphibia
Amphibious
Amplifier
Anakin
Anal
Analog
Android
Andromeda Strain
Angst
Angsty
Ankle Biter
Animal
Animal Instinct
Anime
Anonymity
Anorexia
Ant Man
Anthrax

All-Bran

(AWL-bran)

We are what we eat. There is no more earthy, life-sustaining nutrient than bran, the very fiber of life itself. Tough yet tender, 'All Bran' can show it's not just about brains and brawn…it can also be about bran!

Anti-Nausea
Antifa
Antihistamine
Antique White
Anyway
Apache
Apartheid
Apocalypse Now
Apology
Apostrophe
Apotheosis
Applebee
Applejack
Apples to Apples
Appointment
Apprentice
Aquafina
Aqualung
Aquarium
Arachnophobia
Aretha Franklin
Arial
Arial Bold
Ark
Armageddon
Arrested Development
Arrhythmia
Arschlochwinkel
Arsenal
Arsenic
Artichoke
Artifice
Artificial
Artisanal
Artisanal Chocolate
ASAP
A$AP
Aside
Asphyx
Asteroid
Asthma
Astroglide
Astroglide Water Based
Atheist
Atomic
Attila
Audacity
Authority
Avalanche
Avant-Garde
Avatar
Avenger
AWOL
Axe
Axios

Arschlochwinkel

(ARSH-lohk-winkuhl)

A hiking and climbing area at the foot of the Dachstein Mountains in the Salzkammergut region of Austria, found almost exclusively on hiking maps.

B

B'dazzled
Baba Ganoush
Baba Ram Dass
Baby Melon
Babylon 5
Backlash
Bad Bunny
Baddie
Badoo
Bae
Bæst
Baguette
Bait
Bake Off
Bald Twit
Baldur
Ballboy
Baller
Balm
Balmy
Bandit
Bang
Banger
Bangor
Banjax
Barber
Barbie
Barbiturate

Barefoot
Barf
Barista
Barracuda
Basic
Basic Bitch
Baste
Battleship
Bauhaus
Bazooka
Bazooka Joe
Beanie Baby
Beaujolais
Beaver
Bed Bugs
Bedlam
Beamer
Beep Beep
Beep Boop Borp Beep Borp
Beeper
Beer
Beerbong
Beetlejuice
Before
Behappy
Beige
Beluga
Ben-Hur
Bender
Benjamins
Benzo
Beowulf
Berserk
Berth
Bespoke
BestBuy
Beta-Blocker
BFF
Bhoy
Big Baby
Big Bang
Big Bird
Big Booty
Big Deal
Big Johnson
Big Oil
Bigfoot
Biggie
Bilingual
Biloxi
Binge
BiodegradableBionic
Birkenstock
Birth
Birthday
Birthday Cake
Bismarck
Bismol

B'dazzled

(buh-DA-zld)

Let's start right at the top of our 'B' List, with 'B'dazzled', no doubt a top name contender. As soon as you hear it, the name 'hits you' viscerally. Your wondrous child is certainly born B'dazzled—and anyone who encounters them will also immediately experience this effect.

Big Booty

(big BOO-tee)

Our shared popular culture is a rich source for naming possibilities. The name 'Big Booty' derives from a song by Atlanta's own rap sensation, Gucci Mane. It's a classic song on his fourteenth studio album, *Woptober II*, of 2019. On this track, the Southern maestro collaborates with songstress Megan Thee Stallion to give us Big Booty. Is there a hallmark of physical anatomy and personal beauty more celebrated today than Big Booty? We think not. And it's a name befitting an infant that can gracefully continue on to serve its owner into adulthood.

Bismutite
Bisque
Bitch, Give it a Rest
Bitch, Stop Playin'
Bitche
Bite
Biter
Black Bean
Black Mirror
Black Ops
Black-Owned
Blackjack
Blam!
Blanched
Blank
Blanket
Blarney
Blast
Blatant
Blather
Blaze
Blazes
Bleach
Bleep
Blenda
Blendable
Blink
Blitz
Blitzer
Blitzkrieg
Blizzard
BLK
Blogger
Blotter
Blow Hole
Blunderbore
Blue Jean
Blue Meanie
Blue State
Bluff
Blunt
Blur
Blush
Bluto
BMW
Boar's Head
Boaty McBoatface
Boba Fett
Bodega
Body Bag
Bog
Boggart
Boggle
BOH-buh Fett
Boi
Bollocks
Bombshell
Bondo

Bondo Body Filler
Bondoux
Boneless
Bonk
Boo Boo
Boobie
Boobrie
Booger
Boogie
Boomer
Bootie
Booty Royale
Bora Bora
Borax
Bordella
Bordello
Boss
Bostitch
Bot
Botch
Boujee
Bounce
Bounty
Boy Scout
Brain Rot
Brain Surgeon
Brand
Brand Name
Brawny
Brazilian
Brazilian Wax
BRB
Bread Crumb
Breed
Brick
Bright Yellow
Brillo
Brita
Broken Record
Brolly
Brolic
Bromance
Bronze
Brot
Brow
Bruh
Brut
Brutus
BTW
Bubble
Bubble Buddy
Bubble and Squeak
Buckaroo
Bucket
Bucket List
Buckethead
Buckshot Rhonda
Buffalo Bill

Buffy
Bugger
Bulletproof
Bumble
Bump
Bumper
Buoy
Buoyant
Burger
Burger King
Burnt Umber
Bushy
Bussin'
Buster
Butch
Buwch
Buttah
Butter
Butterball
ButterBalm
Butterfinger
Buttermelt
Büüger
Buzz
Buzzcocks
Buzzer Beater
Buzzy
Bykker
Byronic
Byte
Byter
Byzantine
Byzantius

C

Cabal

Cactus

Cadet

Cadmium

Cain

Calamity

Calamity Jane

Caligula

Call of Duty

Camaro

Camry

Canary

Candide

Candle

Candyman

Cannabinoid

Cannabinoid Hyperemesis

Cannabinoid Receptor

Cannabis

Canned Heat

Cannibal

Cannonball

Canon

Canyon

Capacity

Capone

Call of Duty

(kaal uhv DOO-tee)

Certainly, there is no more honorable path for a child to ultimately fulfill than to honor the glory of his/her/their own nation through a life of service, whether it means joining the Army, Navy, Air Force, Marines—or even the Coast Guard. The name 'Call of Duty' reflects the deepest level of brave commitment to this most noble destiny.

Carte Blanche

(KAART blanch)

A beautiful name which, when pronounced aloud, celebrates its French heritage. 'Carte Blanche' immediately describes free will, the absolute authority to act on one's instincts or whims, without restrictions from family, coworkers, or potential rivals. More literally, in English translation, it simply means 'blank paper', celebrating the notion that each of us is born unique, a document of sorts, awaiting its own distinct personal signature.

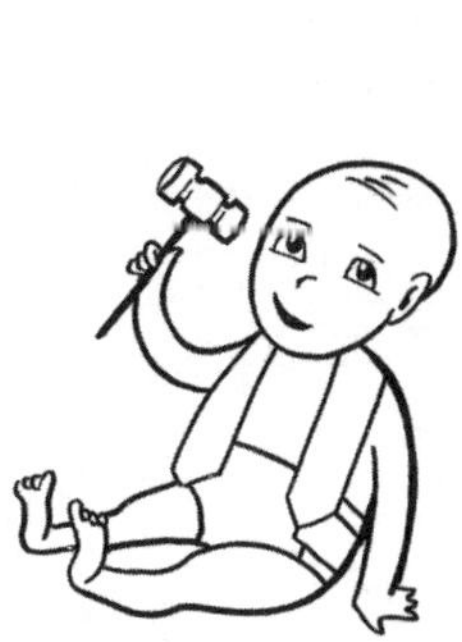

Capri-Sun
Captain America
Captain Underpants
Captain's Log
Car Wash
Cardiac
Carjacker
Carrot
Carte Blanche
Casanova
Cascade
Cataclysm
Catnip
Caucasian
Cavity
CD ROM
Celebrity
Cesarean
Chainsaw
Chainsmoker
Chamber
Changeling
Chaos
Chapter
Chapter One
Chapter Two
Charlie Watts
Charmin
Charro!
Chasm
Chastity
ChatGPT
Chatter
Chalk
Cheaper
Cheat Code
Checkers
Cheeks
Cheeky
Cheerio
Cheers!
Cheez-It
Chernobyl
Cherub
Chestnut
Chex
Chex Mix
Chick Magnet
Chihuahua
Child Soldier
Chile
Chill
Chill Out
Chime-In
China White
Chinese Folklore
Chipotle
Chip

Changeling

(CHAYNJ-lihng)

This name brings with it certain historical challenges. Deriving from Celtic and Norse mythologies, it originally meant a fairy or supernatural creature swapped for a stolen human child, often strange and sickly in appearance. However, in today's contemporary parlance, it can take on a whole new meaning: a child willing to change in accordance with his/her/their own destiny, which could mean gender, or religion, or occupation. An expression of the ultimate willingness to inhabit freedom of spirit and will.

Chihuahua

(chu-WAA-wuh)

One's first association may, understandably, be to the beloved breed of dog: a miraculous and playful miniature miscreant in our midst. A chihuahua is known for being fiercely loyal and often possessing a large, tempestuous personality, despite their delicate build. (Be careful, however, as giving your baby the name 'Chihuahua' may lead to a child prone to barking and nipping.) The name can also serve as a proud declaration of Mexican heritage, as it comes from a royal Spanish city, which rose to power in the 18th century and today attracts both tourists and scholars.

Chips
Chlamydia
Chloride
Choke
Chopper
Christmas Pie
Chrome
Chuck E. Cheese
Chuck Roast
Chucky
Chuffy
Chug Life
Chum Bucket
Chumilingus
Chunk
Chunky Salsa
Chutzpah
CIA
Cialis
Cinderblock
Cipro
Cirque du Soleil
Cisco Kid
Citizen
Citroën
Clairvoyant
Clamato
Clam
Clambake
Clanker
Claritin
Claritin Generic
Claustrophobia
Clause
Claws
Cleanse
Cleanser
Cleavage
Clinker
Clobber
Clog
Clone
Clorox
Cloud
Cloudy
Clout
Clunker
Cluster
Clytemnestra
Coal
Cocaina
Coconut
Codeine
Codex
Cologne
Colonel Birdseed
Colossus
Coma

Combat Zone
Comma
Concealer
Conception
Confetti
Congo Pink
Conjoindia
Conjoined
Continuum
Converse
Conversion
Cookies
Coolie
Coochie
Cooter
Cootie
Cornsilk
Corporation
Corpse
Corpse Bride
Cosmic Latte
Country Crock
Couscous
CoverGirl
COVID-19
Coyote
Crabapple
Cracker Jack
Cradle
Crafty
Crash
Crave
Crawl
Crawler
Cream
Creamy
Creation
Creed
Creep
Creeper
Cretin
Crevice
Cringe
Crisis
Crisp X
Critter
Croaker
Crock Pot
Cronch
Crossbones
Crucible
Cruella
Crumb
Crush
Crustacean
Crybaby
Crypta
Ctrl+Alt+Del

Conception

(kuhn-SEP-shn)

A celebration of the biological act itself: 'Conception'. Biblical, profound, and ultimately sexy.

Cypher

(SAI-fr)

What is a cypher? The word is a question—a question that seems to ask a question. Coming from cryptography, it means a special code. In the case of your child, this code lies in waiting—to be unlocked and discovered, with its true meaning revealed in the future. It is the name of fate itself. It has also become a known moniker in the hip-hop community, denoting a rapper who is able and willing to perform freestyle. Here is a name—'Cypher'—that is mysterious, exciting, with copious possibilities.

CTRL+COMMAND
Cucumba
Cucumber
Cuddle
Cue Card
Cuisinart
Cujo
Cumbria
Cupcake
Curd
Curious George
Curveball
Custom
Cutlet
Cutter
Cy Young
Cyanide
Cyanidia
Cyber
Cyberpunk
Cybersex
Cyborg
Cyclizine
Cyclone
Cypher

D

D-Struct
Dada 5000
Damage
Damaged
Dank
Dannon
Dap
D.A.R.E
Dark
Dark Salmon
Darth
Darwin
Dasani
Data
Date
DayQuil
DEWALT
Deadass
Deadpool
Deadpool 2
Death Glare
Deathmask
Decadence
Deep
Deep Impact
Deep Space

Deep Taupe

(deep tohp)

This is one of several names we have selected based on the experience of a very special color: in this case, a dark, stately brown that may carry a hint of gray. So this name can subtly assert a proud ethnic heritage, perhaps of ancient African origin. Today, the color is often paired with brighter hues. In a world where we have come to celebrate our shared diversity, this homage to color itself reminds us of who we really are—and where we possibly came from.

Deep State
Deep Taupe
Deetz
Defense
Defiance
Defiant
Delicatessen
Deluge
Delulu
Delusion
Demon
Deviant
Dialogue
Diazepam
'Did He Know?'
Diesel
Diet
Different
Digital
Dim
Dim Gray
Dimples
Diner
Dinghy
Dingo
Dirt Devil
Diss
Distant
Diva
Dixie Chick
Dizzy
Django
DMX
DNA
Do-Si-Do
Do-Si-Don't
Dodger
Dollar
Dollar General
Dolomite
Dolphin
Don Juan
Don Julio
Don Quixote
Donut
Doobie Brother
Dood
Doom
Dope
Dopplegänger
Dorita
Dorito
Dossier
Double-Negative
Doublemeat
Down Low
Downtempo
Doxx

Dr. Pepper

(DOK-tuh PEP-er)

It takes audacity to name one's self, or one's child, 'Dr'. That is a distinction of education, intellectual authority, and dominance. In sports, think of 'Dr. J'. (Notice: A number of our suggested names carry this distinctive appellation.) Yet, 'Dr. Pepper' is truly something special. This well-known miraculous elixir is, in fact, concocted from 23 distinct ingredients to elicit a unique, carbonated beverage refreshment. First invented in 1885 in Waco, Texas, in an old country corner drugstore, Dr. Pepper first gained national attention at the 1904 World's Fair in St. Louis. It's more than just one of America's oldest brand names; it means your baby is sure to become its own patented brand of spicy treat.

Dukakis

(doo-KAA-kuhs)

At first glance, an unlikely baby name, indeed. An homage to Michael Dukakis, the 1970s-era US governor of Massachusetts. We now remember 'Dukakis' the national firebrand, a politician who boldly embraced his own Greek and Aromanian bloodlines. He was our first Greek Orthodox major-party US presidential candidate, running as the Democratic nominee in 1988 against Republican George H. W. Bush and his running mate, Dan Quayle. Dukakis's landslide loss has subsequently only added to his luster as a true renegade of both spirit and belief.

Doxxing
Dr. Dre
Dr. Fauci
Dr. Faustus
Dr. J
Dr. No
Dr. Pepper
Dr. Pyckle
Dr. Who
Dr. Zaius
Drab
Drama
Dramamine
Drano
Dread
Dregs
Dremel
Dribble
Drifter
Dristan
Drive-In
Drogyn
Drone
Druid
DUI
Dukakis
Dümmer
Dune
Dungaree
Dungeon Master
Duracell
Duraflame
Dusty
Dusty Carpet
Dweller
DWI
Dybbuk
Dynamite
Dysfunction
Dystopia

E

E. Pluribus
Earl of Sandwich
Earnest
Earp
Earthquake
East Caldwell
Eau de Toilette
Ebola
Echo
Eczema
Edsel
Eerie
Eggnog
Eggo
Eggshell
Ego
Eh
eHarmony
El Jefe
Elaan
Electric Purple
Element
Elf
Ellipse
Ellipses
Elmer's

Earl of Sandwich

(url of SAND-wich)

This suggestion may come as a bit of a stretch. Who would name their own dear child 'Earl of Sandwich'? But hold on, just consider this: Firstly, you are immediately elevating them to nobility, in the British definition, to 'Earldom'. They may henceforth be properly addressed as 'My Lord' or 'Your Lordship'. But why the Earl of Sandwich? Simply put, this will put it out there that your child has an incredible appetite for life—and may eventually excel in the culinary arts. (Perhaps this is already a tradition in your family.) Historical background: John Montagu, the 4th Earl of Sandwich, was an 18th-century English nobleman who popularized eating sliced meat between sheets of bread as a way to avoid greasy hands. The rest, as they say, is history. So, eat up! 'I'll have mine Pastrami on Rye!'

Elmo
Emergency
Emerging Artist
Eminence
Emoji
Emote
Emphasis
Empirical
Employee
Empty
En Route
Enema
Entendre
Envelope
Epcot
Epic
Epilepsy
Epiphany
Episode
Erectile
Escalade
Escape
ESPN
ESPY
Estas Borracho?
Et Cetera
Eulogy
Euphemism
Evel
Everyday Hero
Evian
Evil Pony
Evil-Lyn
Excedrin
Excel
Exhumed
Exorcist
Exotica
Expo
Export
Extension
Extra
Extra-Strength
Extract
Extremitus

Empirical

(uhm-PEE-ruh-kl)

This stately and melodic name refers to an often-used but little-understood term. 'Empirical' is a forceful name because it is about the unflinching search for truth–truth that should be based on observation, not on false logic. Logic alone can be artful in its philosophical construction, but it often proves faulty when put to the task in real life. Your child, Empirical, will amass knowledge through bona fide experience, sure to make him/her/them a better person!

Excedrin

(uhk-SEH-druhn)

Some people say that having a baby can give you a migraine. As medicine, 'Excedrin' is designed to alleviate that worry. But that isn't why we are suggesting Excedrin. The name goes deeper. The pharmaceutical geniuses at Bristol-Myers Squibb joined together in 1960 to find a way to address the excess of pain that we all may naturally feel in our lives. It is this phonetic association that we find so appealing: Excedrin to ensure against suffering, a balm to the body—and to the human soul. So inspirational, in fact, that we have included it here.

F

F-Bomb

F8

Fabianite

Fabreze

Fabreze Plug In

Facial

Factoid

Facts

Fade

FAFSA

Fairly

Falafel

Fallopia

Fallout

Fallujah

Falsie

Fam

Family Style

Famine

Fancy Feast

Fang

Fangirl

Fanta

Fantastik

Fap

Fappy

Fallopia

(fuh-LOH-pee-uh)

Your daughter will sound like a goddess from ancient Greece. In fact, her name will be that of a celebrated flower, a subgenus of the buckwheat family. In the kingdom of plants, 'fallopia' is a flowering vine, noted for its distinct, delicate white flowers. Its Japanese strain, *Fallopia Japonica*, is considered one of the top 100 invasive species on the planet. (With beauty can also come aggression.) But that's not why we have chosen the name. Rather, we have done so in homage to a woman's own sacred reproductive anatomy. For it is, of course, the fallopian tube that captures her egg after ovulation, serving as the vessel for its subsequent fertilization by incoming friendly male sperms.

Fancy Feast

(FAN-see feest)

Feline fanatics will surely be tempted by this name selection, as it refers to the most cherished of fare available to our small, furry friends with paws and whiskers. 'Fancy Feast', the name, carries with it several clever double–and even triple–entendres. As a brand, it was first introduced by Carnation, which was later acquired by Nestlé Purina. With such sumptuous flavors as pâté and seafood, it revolutionized life for cats. No longer simple carnivores, cats became gourmets. As a baby name, Fancy Feast is certainly top of the food chain.

Fat Bastard
Fate
Fats
Faust
Faux
Favela
Fawn
FBI
FDR
FDR Drive
Fear
Feast
Feeble
Feldspar
FEMA
Female
Fent
Fentanyl
Fenty
Feral
Fern
FERPA
Ferret
Fertility
Fetish
Fetty
Feucht
Fickmühlen
Fiddler
Fido
Fiesta
FIFA
Fifth
Fila
Filet
Fill
Filler
Fillette
Filter
Final
Final Fantasy VII
Finale
FingerLickin'
Finish
Fire
First Down
Fishizzle
Fist
Five-Minute Abs
Fiver
Fjuckby
Flagyl
Flanjoid
Flashback
Flattop
Flava
Flesh
Flex

Favela

(fah-VEH-lah)

Don't prejudge a very pretty name by its common meaning. When we say 'favela', we naturally think of the Brazilian shantytown, high on a hill above the glistening international metropolis of Rio de Janeiro. It's a place known to be plagued by gangs, drugs, and turf wars. In fact, the site was first named after a 19th-century battle that took place there, when the hill was known for being covered with 'Morro da Favela', a thorny plant named after the Latin *faba* bean. Sure, it's one of the world's toughest places, especially to grow up in, but from such humble origins often comes beauty, strength, and temerity. Nowhere else is overcoming human adversity so prized—and rewarded. That gives 'Favela' memorable staying power.

Fling
Flippant
Flipper
Flippin'
Flomax
Flonase
Flood
FLOTUS
Flowerbomb
Fluency
Fluidmaster
Fluke
Fluorescent
Fluoride
Flushing
Fly
Fly Trap
Fo Shizzle
Foam
Foamy
Fogger
Folgers
Foliage
FOMO
Font
Foordi
Forceps
Fore
Forever
Formula
Fortnite
Foundation
Four
4th Wall
40 Dollars
Fox
Fozzie
Fracture
Fragile
Fragrance-Free
Frankenhooker
Frankenstein
Freaked
Freckles
Freddy Krueger
Freddy Mercury
Free Will
Freestyle
Frenzy
Freudian
Friction
Fried
Frisbee
Friskie
Frodo
Frontal Lobe
Frostbite
Fruit Loop

Fluke

(flook)

This name's current meaning is associated with the common phrase, 'a fluke of luck'. That means that something good happened unexpectedly. It's an idiom that derives from the 19th-century game of billiards, made popular among British and American players. In the case of a baby name, 'Fluke' could celebrate the result of an unplanned pregnancy, perhaps one experienced later in life. Or, alternately, the unlikely reward of IVF, in vitro fertilization. Such a happy outcome could certainly be called Fluke or 'Fluky'. Try to forget that Fluke is also the name of a peculiarly flat fish of the North Atlantic Ocean, in fact, a flounder.

Fugazi

(foo-GA-zee)

Sure, Italian slang words can sometimes come across as crass, or even rude. Particularly 'fugazi', which means something false, bogus, or inauthentic. Yet that's part of the fun and folly of this suddenly popular unisex moniker. Now, we know 'Fugazi' as the name of a legendary post-punk hardcore band. And Fugazi is also the name of a trendy retail apparel brand, with boutiques on New York City's Lower East Side and at the Los Angeles Art District's Dover Street Market. Just say it: Fugazi. It's irresistible. Are you worried about having a 'Mob Baby'? Fuhgeddaboudit.

FUBAR
FUBU
Fuchs
Fuchsia
Fugazi
Fukah
Fukushima
Full Throttle
Fullmetal
Fumble
Fungo
Fungo Bat
Fungus
Fuqaha
Fury
Fusion
Fussy
Futura
FYI

G

G-Spot
G-String
G.I. Joe
G'day Mate
Gabapentin
Gabagool
Gaddafi
Gadget
Gait
Gallows
Gambit
Gander
Gangster
Gargoyle
Gas-X
Gate
Gator
Gecko
Gel
Gender
Gene Pool
General Patton
Generation X
Generic
Generic Version
Generic Xanax

G-Spot

(JEE-spaat)

Happily, there is more to sexual reproduction than just making babies. This name celebrates that.

GIF

(gif or jif)

'GIF', you can say it with a hard 'G' or a soft 'G'; the choice is yours. Based on a tech-savvy acronym, GIF stands for 'Graphics Interchange Format'. We urge you to retain the capitalization in your baby's naming to preserve authenticity of meaning. For those of you who may already be digital creators, you know that a GIF is either a static image or a short looping animation. They are used to convey humor or emotion and, especially, to express delight. Also, like a perfect child, a GIF won't make a sound. Your little boy or girl will be arriving platform-ready, whether it be for Instagram, X, or something wholly new that we haven't even imagined yet.

Genome
Genre
Gerber
Geritol
Gerund
Getabeer McCheeks
Get Over It
Ghost
Ghostie
Ghostly
Ghoul
GIF
Giggle
Giggles
Gimp
Gimpy
Glam
Glargine
Glaze
Glazed Donut
Glee
Glipzide
Gloaming
Gloat
Gloryhammer
Glow
Glow Reviver
Glue
Glurge
Gnocci
GOAT
Göbekli Tepe
Goblet
Goblin
Godzilla
Golden Poppy
Goldenrod
Goldfinger
Goldilocks
Golem
Goliath
Gonzo
Goo Gone
Goober
Good & Plenty
Good Boy
Goodbye
Goodfella
Good Humor
Goofy
Goofy Goober
Google
Goosebump
GoPro
GORD
Gore
Gorilla
Gorilla Glue

Gloaming

(GLOW-muhng)

Looking for mood? Look no further. 'Gloaming' is a name based on an extraordinarily beautiful physical phenomenon: the perception of light in a twilight landscape. John Keats, leading British Romantic poet born in the late 18th century, loved the term. He used gloaming to metaphorically describe melancholic feelings as provoked by misty atmospheres, particularly in his well-known narrative work *La Belle Dame sans Merci*, in which a knight becomes enchanted with a fairy woman. Some parents will name their daughter 'Autumn'. Try Gloaming instead. It's far more reaching and effective. And glamorous.

Göbekli Tepe

(gow-BEH-klee TEH-puh)

In Turkish, it means 'Potbelly Hill'. Yet, in its original form, it's much more powerful: 'Göbekli Tepe'. There is so much that is original and inspiring about this sacred place name of preagricultural-era monumental buildings. It's said to be at least twelve thousand years old. Older than the great Egyptian pyramids of Giza, perhaps the most ancient known civilization in the world. This has naturally led people to think that Göbekli Tepe is all that remains from a forgotten culture, or possibly is even the work of extraterrestrials. The Bible's Book of Genesis suggests Göbekli Tepe may be the final resting place of Noah's Ark. You can not only honor your child with this portentous name, Göbekli Tepe, you can also casually refer to him/her/them as 'Pre-Pottery Neolithic'. Let's get back to where it all first began!

Gossip Girl
Goth
Gourd
Government Cheese
Government Mule
Granite
Granny Smith
Grasshopper
Grateful
Gravedigger
Gravity
Gravy Train
Great
Gremlin
Grendel
Grim
Grim Reaper
Grinder
Grindr
Grizzly
Groan
Groan Ass
Groomer
Grown
Grown Ass
Grrl
Grub Killer Plus
Grubhub
Grudge
Gruel
GTA
Gucci
Guess
Guggenheim
Guise
Gun Crazy
Gunner
Gunk
Gunmetal
Gunner
Gutterball
Gwrgi
Gyatt
Gypsum

Guggenheim

(GOO-guhn-hime)

20th-century art maven Peggy Guggenheim boldly asserted: 'I was a liberated woman long before there was a word for it'. Such was the spirit of the dynasty of the great Guggenheim family, known for their generous philanthropy. One of them, Benjamin Guggenheim, actually went down with the *Titanic* in 1912. (He was said to have 'put women and children first' into the scarce few available lifeboats.) Of course, it is Solomon R. Guggenheim who funded the modern art museum that bears his name on New York's Fifth Avenue. Designed by genius architect Frank Lloyd Wright, it still stands as a hallmark of modernity and avant-garde thinking. Any child named 'Guggenheim' will no doubt garner respect and admiration.

H

Hacker

Hackery

Hades

Hag

Haggis

Hail

Hail Mary

Half-Life

Halite

Halloween

Halo

Hamas

Hamlet

Hammer

Hammerhead

Hammy

Hamster

Handshake

Hannah Montana

Hannibal

Hanoi

Hansel

Happening

Happen

Happy Ending

Hard

Hail Mary

(hayl MEH-ree)

This respectful religious name refers to a traditional Catholic prayer to the Virgin Mary. But we Americans more often think of 'Hail Mary' with regard to our glorious national game of football. Hail Mary represents the ultimate miracle in sports. The name's use for this purpose was first noted at such Catholic institutions as Indiana's University of Notre Dame. The Hail Mary was popularized for all on December 28, 1975, during an NFL playoff game between the Dallas Cowboys and the Minnesota Vikings. Dallas quarterback Roger Staubach threw a 50-yard, fourth down Hail Mary pass to teammate Drew Pearson in the final minutes of the game. If you are asked about your choice of the name, simply tell people it is a recognition of 'the intercession of God'.

Hannah Montana

(HA-nuh maan-TA-nuh)

As a general rule, we have tried to avoid including too many celebrity names. (Historically, celebrity names have sometimes been misused—and have gone terribly wrong: Such was the case with serial killer John Wayne Gacy [1942–1994].) However, in the case of 'Hannah Montana', we feel compelled toward inclusion. After all, is there a more joyful and ebullient name than Hannah Montana, the alter ego character of our young songbird Miley Cyrus? Introduced by the Disney Channel series (which ran from 2006–2011), the name combines 'Hannah', meaning 'grace', with 'Montana', a US state that represents the extra-large spirit of the American West. If you choose Hannah Montana for your child, you too will be celebrating family, identity, and possible future fame.

Hard Launch
Hardware
Harpo
Hashtaag
Hashtag
#
Haunted
Hawk Tuah
Hawk Tuah Girl
Hazard
Haze
Hazing
Hazy
He Had a Name
Heartfelt
Heathers
Heazlewoodite
Heftier
Hefty
Heineken
Heist
Hell Girl
Hellcat
Hellhound
Hello Kitty
Hellraiser
Hells Angel
Helvetica
Hematite
Hennessey
Herbie
Hermaphrodite
Hermaphroditta
Hermphroditti
Heroic
Herself
Hesitant
High Fructose
Highkey
Highway
Hijab
Himself
Hinge
Hippie Chick
Hiroshima
Hobnob
Hoboken
Hodgepodge
Home Alone 2
Home Improvement
Homebody
Homie
Homophone
Honey Lemon
Honey Trap
Honky
Hoodoo
Hoof

Helvetica

(hel-VET-ih-kuh)

We know Helvetica to be the most elegant and sophisticated of modern typefaces. The distinct Helvetica sans-serif font was designed by the Swiss in the late 1950s and became ubiquitous in the 1960s with its use in US corporate advertising and advanced book design. The name 'Helvetica' itself is derived from *Helvetia*, the Latin name for the geographical location that is now Switzerland. Smart, clean, and simple. Such are virtues we could only pray for in a child.

Hooker
Hooky
Hooray!
Hooter
Hoover
Hops
Hirohito
Horsehead
Hoser
Hostage
Hostess
Hot Drop
Hot Magenta
Hot Stuff
Hot Tub
Hound
Hourglass
Hovercraft
Howitzer
Howl
Howling
Hubba Bubba
Hubba Hubba
Hug
Hugh Mungus
Hulk
Human Head
Human Torch
Hummus
Humpty
Hung
Hung Hom
Hurricane
Hurler
Hush Money
Huzz
Huzzah!
Hydraboost
Hydrokenoralsonite
Hyena
Hype
Hyperbole
Hyperdimension
Hyperspace
Hypothetical
Hysteria
Hyundai

Hugh Mungus

(hyoo MUHNG-guhs)

'Hugh Mungus' is quite direct as a name. And, yes, it can operate as a pun for an extra-large baby. It was the taken name of a noted British professional wrestler. But only later did the name Hugh Mungus enter popular folklore. It happened with a public incident in 2016. Seattle resident and public advocate Rudy Pantoja Jr. was leaving a town hall meeting where he had defended the local police. He was confronted by radical feminist and activist Zarna Joshi, who demanded his name, on camera. He responded, 'I'm Hugh Mungus'. She screamed that she was being sexually harassed. The clip went viral on YouTube. (Both parties survived.)

Hype

(hipe)

Need we say more? Definitely worth the hype.

I

'I Can't Believe It's Not Butter'
iCarly
I, Claudius
'I'm With Stupid'
Ibuprofen
Icarus
ICE
Ice Ice Baby
Icebreaker
Iced
Ichiban
Iconic
Id
Idi Amin
Igloo
IKEA
Illeism
Illuminati
Ima Doctor
IMAX
Imitation
Immortal
Impact
Impala
Import
Impossible

Icarus

(I-kr-uhs)

'Icarus' is a wonderful name that comes to us from Greek mythology. Icarus, the son of 'Daedalus', fashioned himself a pair of wings using feathers and wax so that he could escape from prison. When he dared to fly too close to the sun, against his father's previous warnings, he fell into the sea and drowned. So why is Icarus a hero to us today? And why should you name your child after him? Well, the name itself is beautiful and evocative. It now belongs to a cautionary tale that we hold dear about youthful recklessness. If Icarus had nothing else, he had ambition, fearlessness, and—dare we say—balls. (Hey, 'Balls' could be a good name, too.) 'Icarus, don't fly too high'.

Index

(IN-deks)

This suggestion may seem unassuming at first, but 'Index' holds great potential. It's completely unisex, especially in its sound: *Index*. It's wholly androgynous, also, in its cultural implications. Currently rare as a name, it is gradually slipping into usage. It comes from Latin, where it means 'pointer' and therefore wields a strong sense of purpose. As a noun, it has a stately elegance: the stock market index. As a verb, it suggests swift action: the making of a list. Not surprisingly, often a list of *names*. Talk about 'meta'! Some people have a lot of personality. Others have a lot of 'indexicality'.

Impreza
In-N-Out
Inbetweener
Inchworm
Incidental
Incredible Hulk
Index
Indignant
Indignity
Indoor Voice
Inevitable
Inferno
Infinity
Influence
Influencer
Infodump
Informant
Informercial
Innocent
Insta-Flo
Instant
Instant Karma
Insulin
Integra
Interastral
Intern
Invasion
Inverse
Invisible
Irish Potato
Irish Spring
Iron Maiden
Ironic
Ironica
Ironicubus
Irony
Irresistible
Isis
Itchy
Itsmyluckyday
Itt

Irish Potato

(AI-ruhsh PUH-tay-tow)

Without the Irish potato, or lack thereof, there would have been no Irish Potato Famine in the mid-19th century. A huge wave of Irish immigrants came to the US. Without them, we wouldn't have all the Irish cops, firemen, writers, musicians, and comedians among us today who make our country great. And no mighty Kennedy family political dynasty. Yes, the potato may be humble, but its cultural impact is significant, indeed. The name 'Irish Potato' commonly refers to the white potato, *Solanum Tuberosum.* In Appalachia, the name Irish Potato has been shortened to 'Arsh Potato', which makes for a spirited regional variation of its own.

J

Ja Rule
Jack Daniels
Jack the Ripper
Jackhammer
Jam
Jammy
Jane Doe
Jawn
Jaws
Jazzberry Jam
Jdate
Jeezuz
Jeffrey Epstein
Jekyll
Jell-O
Jelly
Jellybean
Jerry Garcia
Jersey
Jezebel
Jif
Jiffy
Jigger
Jim Beam
Jim Jim
Jimbo

Jizzakh

(jiz-ZAK)

'Jizzakh' is a magical and little-known city in the Central Asian country of Uzbekistan. Jizzakh may alternatively be spelled 'Jizzak' or 'Jizzax'. (Both sound jizzy *and* jazzy.) All these derive from the Uzbek, *Jizzax*. The name serves as an homage to the riches of the Zarafshan Valley, known for its goat-cheese curds and extra-large breads. The city was once a fortification of sorts, an 'iron gate' along the Silk Road trading route. In its modern incarnation, it is proudly home to the Jizzakh Polytechnic Institute and the Jizzakh State Pedagogical Institute. Most distinct is the Soviet-era Zamin Sanitarium. Even today, it still takes an intrepid adventurer to make it to exotic Jizzakh with its alluring and unusual name.

Jughead

(JUHG-hed)

Take a trip to the Golden Age of comic books and throwback American innocence with this all-time classic honorific name, 'Jughead'. It belongs to a central character in the beloved Archie series. Jughead is the nickname of Forsythe Pendleton Jones, III. He was first introduced in *Pep Comics* no. 22, of December 1941. Jughead is the best friend of Archie Andrews and hangs around with Betty Cooper, Veronica Lodge, and Reggie Mantle. Jughead is by far the most distinct of this Riverdale High crew. He's a proto–Beat Generation renegade: a witty, cynical nonconformist. Jughead, the name, most likely refers to his elongated head shape, long nose, and half-closed eyes. He wears a 'whoopee cap', crown-like in its shape (this distinct cut-felt apparel item is, in fact, based on a trend among the 'Jag Heads' youth movement of the day.) He also wears an iconic gray sweater, emblazoned with a large, mysterious letter 'S'. 'Jughead' is highly intelligent and notoriously lazy but with a high metabolism that allows him to eat a lot of cheeseburgers. His aversion to romantic relationships might be called asexual in today's parlance. In all, Jughead is an unexpected prototypical folk hero among us, awaiting rediscovery and recognition.

Jive
Jizzakh
Joan of Arc
Joe Rogan Podcast
John Doe
Johnson
Joyride
Jug Face
Juggernaut
Jughead
Jugs
Juicy Couture
Juicy Fruit
Jumbo
Jumbotron
Jungian
Jungle Boy
Jurassic World
Just Do It
Just Larry
Just Shoot Me!
Justify

Jungian

(YUHNG-ee-uhn)

The Swiss psychologist Carl Jung is a venerated historical figure like Sigmund Freud, but a lot hipper. His New Age theories and terminologies continue to beguile us today. It was Jung who coined the term 'synchronicity'. He also gave us our contemporary concept of 'collective unconscious', describing a psyche shared by all humans. We like 'Jungian' as a name. You can say, 'She was a Jungian'. Or, 'She spoke in Jungian terms'. Jung was obsessed with individuation and divided all people into four major archetypes: 'persona', 'shadow', 'animal', and 'animus' (each of these terms makes for a good name in itself). Of course, 'Jung' originally comes from the German for 'young'. Perhaps you recall the 1968 hit record by Gary Puckett & The Union Gap:

> Jung Girl
> Get out of my mind
> My love for you is way out of line
> Better run, girl
> You're much too *Jung*, girl

K

K
K.O.
Kaamos
Kaatialite
Kaboom!
Kamaro
Kampfire
Kansas
Kaput
Karen
Karma
Kato Kaelin
Kato Kaitlyn
Kawasaki
Ke$ha
Keebler
Keener
Keep Honking
Kelpie
Ken
Kerfuffle
Kermit
Ket
Ketamine

Kaamos

(KAH-mos)

'Kaamos' is the Finnish name for 'polar night', a period of the long winter months when the sun does not rise above the horizon. It's not pitch-black; rather, it is the 'blue hour' of twilight—nature at its most haunting. Perhaps this is why Kaamos was later adopted as the name of a Swedish death metal band. In Lapland, kaamos is a mental state. *The Dictionary of Contemporary Finnish* tells us that the term is synonymous with life-gazing and examining the unknown spaces of the unconscious mind.

Kelpie

(KEL-pee)

The Scottish 'kelpie' is derived, most likely, from such words as *cailpeach* or *colpach*, meaning 'heifer' or 'colt'. It is now accepted as a common name for a mythical shape-shifting water spirit found in Celtic folklore. It can take the form of a male human, a female human, or a horse. A kelpie is said to haunt Scottish lochs and rivers. Parents long used the legend of the kelpie to warn their children of the dangers of drowning. But you can use it as a bold assertion of your Scottish heritage, or as a way of saying that your child is a 'monster' (we only mean that in the good sense).

Ketamine

(KEH-tuh-meen)

Ketamine is a powerful dissociative anesthetic commonly used by doctors and veterinarians. Yet some people also have come to think of it as a magical elixir, a door to the human psyche. Ketamine first gained its popular reputation when it was taken up by 'club kids' at nightclubs such as New York City's notorious Limelight in the 1990s. After ingesting it, revelers would be 'thrown down the K-Hole', a hedonistic shared psychedelic state. Bonded together, the users enjoyed euphoric, out-of-body experiences. These days, the analgesic has been adopted by vanguard purveyors of integrative alternative medicine, used in controlled settings where its hallucinogenic qualities are considered especially effective in treating depression. If you want, you can use one of its alternate nicknames: 'Special K', 'Vitamin K', or 'Cat Valium'.

KGB
Khaki
Kia
Kid Pro Quo
Kief
Kill Switch
Killz
Kilz
Kimchi
Kinda Gangster
King Kong
Kissimmee
Kit Kat
Kite
Kitten
Klass
Klassehest
Klebb
Klimt
Klingon
Klitten
Klonopin
Klout
Klutch
Knapsack
Knave
Knobhead
Knock Knock
Knotty
Knuckles
Kommunizm
Koozie
Korky
Korvette
Kraanium
Krackers
Krakatoa
Kraken
Kraków
Krazy Kat
Krenk
Krew
Krill
Krispy Kreme
Krueger
Krylon
Kurma
Kush
Kvetch
Kwikset

Klass

(klas)

'Klass,' also 'Klas' and 'Klaus', is short-form German for the more formal 'Nicholas'. It also comes from Greek roots, meaning 'victory for the people'. In Eastern Ashkenazi Jewish languages, it can refer to a musician, or 'klezmer'. In Czech and Slovak, it can mean 'ear of corn'. Such a myriad of associations! Of course, we like that it actively puns with the English term 'class': 'Your baby's got Klass!' Perhaps this is why Klass has been adopted as a brand name for the popular Aguas Frescas beverage line sold at Walmart and is the name of a popular Haitian vocal supergroup. Klass is catchy and fun. No matter what the context.

Klitten

(KLIT-tun)

Klitten is a charming village in rural Saxony, Germany. Its name reflects its Slavic origins. If you go, don't miss the Museum Margarethenhütte.

Koozie

(KOO-zee)

Koozie, also known as 'Coozy' or 'Cozie', is a snug sleeve designed to thermally insulate drinks in bottles and cans. Loved by sports fans and beachgoers alike, a Koozie may keep a cold drink cold or a hot drink hot. Often, they come in eye-catching colors of foam or neoprene and sport amusing sayings and graphics. As a name, 'Koozie' is darn cute—if we do say so ourselves. Who wouldn't want to be a Koozie?

Krylon

(KRAI-laan)

'Krylon' is, unabashedly, one of the coolest names in this book. It's both futuristic and phonetically satisfying. Any city dweller knows that it's also strongly rooted in the street cred of the urban graffiti art movement, which began in the late 1970s in the South Bronx, at the dawn of hip-hop culture. The name of a spray paint brand, Krylon was the brainchild of Philadelphia businessman Howard E. Koster. In 1947, Koster mused that liquid and gas might be combined to apply paint via aerosol. He borrowed part of the name Krylon from nylon, which had just been invented by the chemical giant DuPont. One of Krylon's early advertising mottos was: 'Krylon can turn old new again'. How appropriate for your infant!

L

Lab Rat
Labis
Lacoste
Lactaid
Lapis Lemon
LASER
Lasik
LASIK
Lassie
Last
Late
Latina
Latino
Latinx
Launch
Lavagirl
Lawn
Lawrence of Arabia
Lawrence of Portland Maine
Lawrence of Staten Island
Layman
Lazarus
Le Freak
Leaf Blower
Leaky
Learner

Lacoste

(laa-KAAST)

'Lacoste' is sporty and classy. A winning combination. With a dash of European sophistication, or, as the French say, élan. Originally, this name was known only as a surname, associated with people who lived near the coast. It rose to prominence as belonging to the French world tennis champion of the 1930s, René Lacoste, who was nicknamed 'the Crocodile'. Now used as a first name, Lacoste stands for luxury, sophistication, and lifestyle. Although retro in its flavor, Lacoste makes 'preppy' cool all over again.

Lawn

(laan)

Yes, at first, 'Lawn' may come across as a little unexpected…even abrupt. But think about it: What is a greater source of all-American pride than our lawn? You could name your child 'Fern', 'Forest', 'Ivy', or even 'Heather'. But why retread such overused clichés? After all, there is nothing more satisfying than a good lawn.

'Lee Harvey Oswald Didn't Act Alone'
Left
LEGO
LEM
Lemur
Leprechaun
Lesbia
Lesbos
Let Us
Let Us Pray
Lethal
Lettuce
Leviathan
Lexapro
Libation
Liberal
Libido
Lickety Split
Lifer
Lil Baby
Lil Bit
Lil Squirt
Lil Wayne
Lilith
Limitation
Limited Edition
Limp Bizkit
Ling Ling John John
Linguist
LinkedIn
LinkedIn Login
Lipitor
Lipps Inc.
Liquid
Liquid Death
Liquid Nails
Liquidate
Liquor Box
Listerine
Lit
Lite
Lithium
Litter
Little Friskie
Little Friskies Paté
Little Friskies Shreds
Liver
Liver Pudding
Llama
Load Bearing
Loaf
Lobster
Lobus
Local
Locust
Login
LOL
Lolita
Lollipop

Leviathan

(luh-VAI-uh-thn)

'Leviathan'. This name is going to be huge! It's legit because it comes from the Bible. But it still carries a lot of contemporary *swag*. Forget the Book of Job, Leviathan immediately references the most massive and magnificent of all of God's creatures: the whale. Moby-Dick has nothing on your kid when he/she/they show up calling themself Leviathan.

Lexapro

(LEK-suh-prow)

'Lexapro'. (Call her 'Lexi!') As millions of ordinary Americans have come to rely on Lexapro as their go-to antidepressant, so we suggest that the name itself be considered by you. We already know it's a proven mood elevator. Let's all leave our anxieties far behind and look forward to a new age of serotonin-tinged, advanced enlightenment. Who knows? Someday our next president could be named Lexapro.

Loophole

(LOOP-howl)

'Loophole' is a name that could keep your child out of a lot of possible future troubles.

Lubriderm

(LOO-bri-derm)

Try to overcome any peculiar associations that the sweet, soft-sounding name 'Lubriderm' may conjure. At its most basic, Lubriderm is really a name that celebrates replenishment. Once you have enjoyed full hydration for between 24 and 48 hours without any attendant greasiness, well, there's really no looking back. Plus, phonetically, Lubriderm just rolls off the tongue.

Lvcifyre

(LOO-si-fire)

Okay, just saying: 'Lvcifyre' may be the *baddest* name in this book. Let's just leave it at that.

Lonely
Looker
Loophole
Lord Byron
Lost
Lotion
Love Interest
Love Thang
Low-Key
lowercase
Lox
Lox Club
Loxy
Lozenge
Lubber
Lubriderm
Lucifer
Lucy
Ludacris
Ludicrous
Luigi
Lumberjack
Luminescence
Lunar
Lunar Landing
Lunar Module
Lust
Lvcifyre
Lyft
Lysol

M

M*A*S*H
Mac
Macabre
Macbeth
Mace
Machine
Mackeral
Mad Max
MADD
Maduro
Magenta Haze
Magica
Magico
Magma
Magnet
Magnet School
Magneta
Magneto
Mahershalalhashbaz
Mail
Mainstream
Majordomo
Makita
Malaise
Malcolm X
Malcolm Y

Magneto

(mag-NEE-tow)

If there is one quality that we all might ask to be gifted at birth, it could well be the gift of magnetism. That's where the name 'Magneto' comes into play. You can actually predetermine this most valuable trait. The heroic name Magneto comes to us from the unlikely world of comic books, but not just any comic books: Marvel's X-Men series is like our contemporary *Iliad* and *Odyssey*. Its universe was first created by the genius team of Stan Lee and Jack Kirby. Magneto, the alias of Erik Magnus, is a brilliant scientist and a revolutionary leader. He can fly, he exhibits extreme magnetism, and he has the ability to astrally project. Importantly, for today's children, he has taught us that being a mutant can be a source of strength and a virtue. Magneto calls mutants *Homo superior*. Over time, Magneto has gone from supervillain to antihero to superhero. Perhaps your child could aspire to such a path.

Malcolm Z
Male
Male Thong
Mallard
Mam Daddy
Mama Tried
Mamzer
Man Cave
Man Eater
Man o' War
Manatee
Mandrake
Maneater
Manic Panic
Manly
Mantis
Mantra
Mao
Mar-a-Lago
Marauder
Mardi Gras
Marfa
Margerine
Marinade
Marmalade
Marquis de Sade
Marshmallow
Martian
Marxist
Mary Poppins
Marzipan
Mascara
Mascot
Mask
Mascara
Massacre
Massive
Mate
Matte
Maumee
Mauve
Maximum
Maximum Purple
Mayo
Mayo Clinic
Mayo Clinic Portal
Mayor McCheese
McJagger
McLovin'
MDMA
Me Too
Mea Culpa
Meaningful Name
Meatbag
Meatball
Meatwad
Mechagodzilla
Meds

Medusa
Mee2
Mega Man
Megadeth
Megalon
Megaton
Melatonin
Mélange
Mellow Apricot
Menace
Menage
Mensch
Meshuggener
Mesopotamia
Messerschmitt
Messi
Met Food
Metallica
Meteor
Methamphetamine
Methy
Mexican Coke
Micro
Micro-Fine
Microbus
Micron
Microwave
Mid
Middie
Middle
Midnight Blue
Midnight Cowboy
Midol
Midwife Crisis
Miele
MILF
Milkshake
Milky Face
Milky Way
Milquetoast
Mimic
Mineral
Mini Wheat
Mini-Me
Minion
Minis
Minivan
Minotaur
Minwax
Miracle Whip
Miracle-Gro
Miraculous
Mire
Mires
Mirror
Misery
Misogyny
Miss Behavin'

Marfa

(MAAR-fuh)

Yes, 'Marfa' is a small, dusty former military town in the middle of the desert in far-west Texas. It's literally the middle of nowhere. Yet Marfa is a beautiful name, one that carries with it a special meaning that will surely resonate with sophisticates of today and tomorrow. In 1971, the town was taken over by Donald Judd, an avant-garde minimalist sculptor from New York City, famous for his industrially produced plywood boxes and stainless steel 'stacks'. Judd transformed the town of Marfa's long-abandoned munitions-manufacturing buildings into a complex of permanent museums. He moved to a nearby ranch himself. Now, Judd's name, as well as the name Marfa, are both synonymous with the highest achievements in contemporary art and design. If you want your daughter to grow up to be a museum curator, art historian, or potential commercial gallery owner, don't call her 'Martha'. Call her Marfa.

McJagger

(muck-JAG-er)

Sly and understated in its humor, 'McJagger' is, of course, an homage to the legendary *The Rolling Stones* frontman, Mick Jagger, our favorite bad-boy imp. 'Jagger' itself is a distinguished Old English surname, likely from West Yorkshire, an occupational term for a carter or a peddler. Can it be, in hindsight, that Mick Jagger was merely a peddler of *Sympathy for the Devil* in his distinct song lyrics? Mick's name is, of course, short for Michael. He's really Michael Philip Jagger. And Jagger itself has already proven itself a popular first name. This new modification, McJagger, only takes it further. By the way, Sir Mick has bequeathed his daughters with some great names of their own: 'Jade', 'Georgia', 'Karis', and 'Elizabeth'. (He also has three sons.) So, be like Mick, and get some *satisfaction.*

Miracle-Gro

(MIH-ruh-kuhl-groh)

Need we say more? 'Miracle-Gro'.

Miss Oginy
Missing
Mist
Mitten
MK Ultra
MMA
Moat
Modernist
Mofo
Moist
Mollusk
Molly
Molten
Mona Lisa
Money Pit
Mongrel
Monster Energy
Moodswing
Moodswinga
Mook
Moolah
Moon Landing
Moonshine
Moped
Mordred
Morphin
Morphine
Mortal Kombat
Mote
Motel
Motormouth
Mother
Mothra
Motivation
Motive
Motrin
Mousse
Moxxi
Mr. Bean
Mr. Cat
Mr. Chewy
Mr. Clean
Mr. Cleen
Mr. Pibb
Mr. Spats
Mr. Squiggles
Mr. T
mRNA
Ms. America
Ms. Puerto Rico
Mrs. Dash
Ms. Steak
Mucinex
Mudtroll
Muff
Muffy
Muggle
Mule

Muffy

(MUH-fee)

'Muffy' is perhaps the preppiest preppy name ever. After all, for some, living in Connecticut is the only choice.

Mullet
Multiplayer
Mummy
Munch
Münchausen
Munchie
Munchies
Munchkin
Muppet
Muscle Shoals
Muse
Musilax
Musk
Mussel
Mustang
Mustard
Mutant
Mutant Ninja
Mutation
Mutator
Mutt
Mutual
My Bad
My Chemical Romance
My Little Pony
Myst
Mysterio
Mystique

N

NAACP

Nada

NAFTA

NAMBLA

Napalm

Narnia

NASA

NASDAQ

Naughty Naughty

Nausea

Nauti

Nebuchadnezzar

Necromancer

Necrophagia

Necrot

Needles

Neighbor

Nemesis

Neon

Neoprene

Nesquick

Nessie

Neuro

Neuro Diversity

Neutrogena

Never

Nausea

(NAA-zhuh)

'Nausea' is really a very pretty name, quite light on the tongue when spoken or whispered aloud. Unfortunately, as you know, the name has negative associations due to its commonly understood meaning. Nausea, after all, is the familiar queasy feeling of being sick to your stomach. We know it from motion sickness, eating rich foods, and—dare we mention—even pregnancy. Yet the name is also distinguished on other terms. It was used by the French philosopher and novelist Jean-Paul Sartre as a famous book title, for his work introducing the concept of existentialism. *La Nausée* was first published in Paris in 1939 and is a novel written in the form of a personal diary. Its protagonist, Antoine Roquentin, is an intellectual who describes how he begins to enjoy an ongoing sensation of 'sweetish sickness'. Perhaps Nausea is best gendered for a girl: 'Nausea be thy name'!

Nemesis

(NEH-muh-suhs)

Some people seem to thrive on adversity, confrontation, and bullying. If you dare give your child this antagonistic name, 'Nemesis', you may be preordaining them to one day become a rich and powerful attorney-at-law!

Never Again II
New Car
Newb
Nexium
Next
Nibble
Nickel
Nickelback
Nicotine
Nicorette
Night Fever
Night Sweats
Nightmare
Nimrod
Ninja
Nintendo
Nipple
Nipples
Nitro
Nivea
No Biggie
No Nut November
No, You
Noggin
Nollie
Nom de Guerre
Nom de Plume
Nomenclature
Non-Silicate
Noob
Noodge
Noodle
Nor'easter
NORAD
Norse
Nosferatu
Nosh
Nostalgia
Not
Nova
Novel
Novella
Noxema
NSFW
NSYNC
Nu Metal
Nudist
Nudnik
Nurse
Nutella
Nutmeg
Nutri-Grain
Nvidia
NXVIM

Noob

(noob)

'Noob', it's so natural. And so friendly. Just Noob.

Nvidia

(uhn-VI-dee-uh)

Nvidia may be the new world leader in artificial intelligence (AI), but your baby could be the new leader in *real* intelligence. To your child, the name 'Nvidia' would pose a most worthy challenge. The word Nvidia originates from the Latin *Invidia*, meaning 'envy'. (Come to think of it, 'Envy' alone would also be nice.)

O

Oar
Obi-Wan
Object
Oblong
Obscura
Ocean Spray
Octagon
Octopus
Octopussy
OD
Oddie
Oddjob
Oedipus
Off!
Offense
OG
Oh, Hell No!
Oh, Henry!
Oh, Bobby!
Ohio
Oil
Oiler
Okay
OkCupid
Okinawa
Oklahoma

Oprah

(OH-pruh)

Fans of the palindrome are fond of pointing out that 'Oprah' spells 'Harpo' backward. You can celebrate our greatest daytime talk-show host and our greatest silent-vaudeville comedian simultaneously: Oprah Winfrey and Harpo Marx, of course.

Olaf
Old Chap
Old Yeller
Oldie
Olive Drab
Olive Garden
Olive Oyl
Omega
Omelette
Omniglot
One-Piece
Onion
Only Fans
Only Option
Onomatopoeia
Onset
Opioid
Oprah
Optimo
Optimus Prime
Orange Peel
Orange Soda
Orbit
Orca
Ore
Oregon
Oreo
Organ
Orgasm
Origin
Ortega
Ortho
Orthodontia
OSHA
Otro
Otzi
Oui
Ouija
Out of Office
Outburst
Outer Space
Outrageous
Outside
Oven Mitt
Overdose
Overdrive
Overrated
Oxi
Oxi Fresh
OxiClean
Oxy
Oxymoron
Oy Vey
Oyster
Ozempic
Ozempic Side Effect
Ozempic User Guide

OSHA

(OH-shuh)

'OSHA'. Please keep the capital letters intact for this acronym's most powerful effect. This way, the name almost screams: 'I care about you' and 'I want to protect you'. Of course, it is inspired by the federal agency. In its original upper-and-lower-case form, the name OSHA has diverse roots and has long been known as a simple, direct, and stylish choice. In Arabic, Osha means 'protection'. In Armenian, Osha means 'little fawn'. In Hebrew, Osha means 'salvation'. For Native Americans, it comes from the 'Osha Root', which is also a name for 'bear'.

Ouija

(WEE-jee)

We are especially high on this entry, 'Ouija'. Seen typeset in print, it has real presence. Said aloud, it is mysterious and ephemeral—almost like a puff of smoke. Its origins may come from the realm of the supernatural. A Ouija Board is a popular board-game activity. The letters and numbers printed on the board 'talk' to its participants through the manipulation of a cursor-like 'paddle'. It works as a kind of spirit communication or automatism of the mind. The parlor game was first introduced in 1891, when, it is said, the board spelled out its own name: Ouija. In fact, Ouija may have been derived from the French *oui* and the German *ja*, both meaning 'yes'.

P

P!nk

Pac-Man

Paciencia

Paddle

Paddy

Painless

Pale Aqua

Pale Dogwood

Palette

Palindrome

Pallet

Palmolive Liquid

Panama Red

Pandemic

Panic

Pansexual

Pansy

Pansy Division

Pansy Seed

Pantera

Pantheon

Pantone Yellow

Panzer

Papyrus

Para Mormon

Para Norman

Parchment

(PAARCH-muhnt)

Life should be a blank sheet of paper, awaiting content, narrative, and description. The most beautiful thing about a new sheet of paper may be the sense of open space that it affords. It inspires ideas, notions, and intentions. It is about the idea itself. The word 'parchment' originated in Turkey, where sheepskins were often used. The brilliant white translucence of parchment is unparalleled. Just think of the term: 'Her skin is like parchment'. If you want a child who is open, honest, and capable of sharing their feelings—transparent—you should start here.

Patchouli

(puh-CHOO-lee)

Patchouli is a distinct scent, deriving from a Southeast Asian mint-family herb leaf. Treasured by the ancients, its earthy, musky aroma is said to have medicinal and insect-repelling properties. In olden days, patchouli traveled the Silk Road trading routes, exchanged pound for pound with gold from European merchants. Here in the US, in the hedonistic 1960s counterculture heyday, hippies embraced patchouli incenses and perfumes as a fragrant declaration of their own freedom and rebellion. So swaddle your baby in cashmere and anoint them forth into our own redolent and aromatized world.

Paradoxe
Parallel
Parallel Life
Parasite
Parchment
Parenthetical
Parrot
Party Jawa
Party Pooper Pants
Party Wagon
Password
Patchouli
Pause
Paw Paw
Pax Romanus
Paxil
Payback
PC
PDF
Peach Fuzz
Peat
Pebbles
Pecker
Peckerhead
Pee Pee
Peel
Peat
Penance
Pepto
Perfume
Peril
Period Piece
Percocet
Perc
Perks
Perp
Perrier
Persona
Personality
PETA
Peter Pan
Petulant
Pex
Pez
Pfft
Pflugerville
Phazm
Phish
Phobia
Phone
Phone Call
Phosphate
Phthalo
Pickles
Piddle
Piddle Pellet
Pierced
Pigment

Pikachu
Pillow
PIN
Piña Colada
Pine
Pine-Sol
PingFang
Pink Pony
Pinkie
Pinocchio
pip pip
Piranha
Pirate
Pisher
Pistachio
Pistol
Pitter Patter
Placebo
Placid
Plain Pie
Planet
Plasticine
Player
Pledge
Plenty
Plotter
Plugrà
Plumper
Plumping
Plush
Pocahontas
Pocahotass
Pocket Rocket
Pockets
Pod
Podcast
Pogo
Pokémon
Pole Dancer
Polo
Poltergeist
Poly-O
Polygon
Polysporin
Pomegranate
Pomp
Pompeii
Pong
Pontoon
Ponyboy
Ponygirl
Poof!
Pookie
Pop-Tart
Poppin'
Poppins
Popstar
Population

PDF

(pee-dee-eff)

PDF stands for 'Portable Document Format'. A name composed of initials alone can be fun and playful or authoritative and distinct. Consider Vice President J. D. Vance or the fictional Texas oil baron J. R. Ewing. But 'PDF'? A *triple* initial? We say, yes! PDF in particular brandishes unmistakable authority. As a document, a PDF is fixed and unchangeable. And the metaphorical associations continue. Any operating system may enjoy a PDF. A PDF fully respects the diversity of our intellectual hardwares and softwares. Certainly, your new baby is 'portable' (thank God) and is an open document of sorts, awaiting imprinting. So go ahead and dare to 'format' them with this bold name selection.

Phish

(fish)

Love them or hate them, devoted followers of the Vermont-born jam band Phish are rapturous in their loyalty and praise. And, yes, 'Phish' was already a name of sorts. Drummer Jon Fishman was called 'Fish' by his friends in college. Once modified with the 'Ph', the name became more distinct, especially typographically, and its own cultural phenomenon. The name has a certain onomatopoeia: It is fun to say.

Phlox

(flaaks)

The name 'Phlox' comes from the Greek, meaning 'flame'. Now we associate it with a distinct family of vibrantly colored flowers, *Phlox ovata* or *Phlox pungens*, for example. Symbolically, Phlox has come to represent harmony, unity, and love. It says, 'Our souls are united' and 'We think alike'. Caution, however: A baby named Phlox is prone to becoming a butterfly or moth magnet.

Poreless
Porkchop
Porky
Porno
Porpoise
Port
Portal
Posse
Possession
Possibility
Post
Post-Modern
Post-Structuralist
Post-Hardcore
Postmortem
POTUS
Powder
PPL
Prank
Prawn
Pre-Post Structuralist
Pretty Bougie
Previous
Previously Owned
Prey
Price
Prickwillow
Primaeval
Primate
Primer
Pringle
Pro Bono
Prodigal Son
Profanity
Project
Proletariat
Prong
Pronoun
Propeller
Propeller Head
Proper
Prototype
Prozac
Prunella
Prussia
Pseudomalachite
Pseudonym
Psychedelia
Psycho
Public Assistance
Puddle
Puddle Phoenix
Puffy
Püke
Pump
Punch
Punchline
Punchy

Pre-Post Structuralist

(PREE-pohst STRUHK-chuh-ruh-list)

Wait, aren't names with *one* prefix difficult enough? Well, yes, but the proper prefix will help to send your child forth into the world vested with power and distinction. You may well ask yourself, 'What the heck is a "post Structuralist"?' Well, we are glad you asked. It's based on a French philosophical movement of the 1960s, spawned by such radical theorists as Jacques Derrida, Roland Barthes, and Michael Foucault. Who doesn't love the French? These dandies ruled our college classrooms with their big ideas. They were challenging fixed structures, favoring deconstruction. How daring! So, why add the *second* prefix, 'pre'? Because we are now looking to break more boundaries, to reach more remarkable truths awaiting us.

Pungent
Punisher
Punt
Puppeteer
Purchase
Purdy
Purina
Purple Mountain Majesty
Purple Rain
Purple Shotty
Purpose
Puritan
Pussy
Putty
Pygmy
Pyramus

Q

Q-Tip
Quail
Quantum Leap
Quark
Quartz
Quasimodo
Que?
Queue
Question
Quibble
Quicksand
Quid Pro Quo
Quikrete
Quintuplet
Quiver
Quorum
Quote
'Quote Unquote'

Quark

(kwork)

What is a Quark? First, we ask you to just step back and consider how cool it sounds when pronounced aloud. It is, in fact, our most fundamental particle, a building block of matter such as protons and neutrons. First theorized in the 1960s, the physicist Murray Gell-Mann discovered the name 'Quark' while reading James Joyce's *Finnegans Wake*, the notoriously difficult 20th-century novel. Joyce wrote: 'Three quarks for Muster Mark!' (The word itself derives from archaic English or German, for 'croak' or 'curds'.) Give your baby a leg up on becoming a future physicist or even a rocket scientist. And, by the way, 'quarks' are said to come in six distinct 'flavors'.

Que

(keh)

'Que' is a versatile expression that can be either French or Spanish, deriving from the original Latin. Imagine a name so bold and simple, spoken in the lilt of a question. It asks all the essentials at once: 'What?', 'Which?', 'Who?', 'How?'

R

Rabies

Rad

RADAR

Radical

Radio

Radiohead

Rage

Raging Bull

Ragout

Ragu

Rah Rah

Raid

Rain

Raisin

Rambo

Ramen

Ramp

Ransom

Rapid-Fire

Rapture

Rapunzel

Rarify

Rarity

Rasputin

Raspy

Rat Fink

Rat Fink

(rat fingk)

'Rat Fink' sounds kind of bad and stupid, no? Perhaps at first, but let's delve into this name's current shared meaning and its growing cultural significance among custom-car and custom-motorcycle aficionados. Rat Fink is a cartoon character created by hot-rodder artist Ed 'Big Daddy' Roth in the 1960s. Rat Fink is a mischievous, grotesque antihero. The name was coined by Roth ironically. For a rat fink is ordinarily a disliked person, whose name derives from 'rat' (a snitch) and 'fink' (an informer). Now, it has come to mean the opposite: a beloved renegade, the hero of California 'Kustom Kulture'.

Rat X
Ratsak
Rattler
Rawhide
Ray Charles
Raya
Razzle-Dazzle
Re-Animator
React
Reactor
Real
Really
Really?
Rebus
Receptor
Recidivism
Recto
Red Baron
Red Bull
Red Devil
Red Lobster
Red Salsa
Red Wheelbarrow
Red Wine
Redacted
Reddit
Redundancy
Redundancy
Reedickyoulus
Reek
Refuge
Refugee
Regrowth
Reichstag
Relax
Released
Remnant
Renault
RENT
Rental
Repeat
Reptile
Repulsion
Rescue
Resurrection
Retro
Retrovir
Reveal
Revenge
Revival
Rhino
Rhode Island
Rhombohedron
Rhombus
Riddick
Riddle
Riff
Rift

Recidivism

(ruh-SI-duh-vi-zm)

'Recidivism' is a mouthful, to be sure, and leans heavily on its Latin origin, *recidivus* (to 'fall back'). It has become a legal and political buzzword, describing a 'falling back' into criminal behavior following a period of incarceration. But honestly, what child isn't repeatedly scolded and told 'Don't do that again'? It's simply human nature. Today, legal advocates are embracing the term recidivism by reversing its meaning. A mark of shame can become a badge of honor. You 'own it'. Then you overcome it. Dare your child to be the one who breaks the cycle. Perhaps he/she/they will be the one to change how our nation is run.

Refugee

(reh-FYOO-jee)

In the 1970s, rocker Tom Petty put it best when he sang: 'You don't have to live like a refugee'. He is singing to an unknown person. But imagine it could be his own child, as he continues: 'Tell me, why you wanna lay there/and revel in your abandon'. Yes, exactly. We know that international refugees have been stigmatized. They have been glorified. And they have been re-stigmatized. Citizens battle in the streets over this. Claim the name 'Refugee' and honor its distinction. After all, somewhere down the line, our parents were all refugees.

Rims
Ringer
Rinso
Riptide
Risky
Rizz
Road Rage
Road Rash
Roadkill
Roadrunner
Robitussin
Robocop
Rocket Scientist
Rodan
Rogue
Roll-On
ROM
Room
Rosé
Rosemary's Baby
Roto-Rooter
Roux
Rowdy
Rowdy Roddy
Rozen
Rubbermaid
Ruckus
Rudder
Ruff Ryder
Ruffian
Ruin
Rumble
Rump Shaker
Rumpelstiltskin
Rümpfle
Runaway
RuPaul
RuPaul Age
RuPaul Net Worth
Rush
Russet
Rust
Rust-Oleum
Rusty Hinges
Rusty Red
Rye Toast
Ryobi

Ruckus

(RUH-kuhs)

Are you brave enough to raise a 'Ruckus'? We challenge you. The name, still rarely used, was born as a combination of English and American idiomatic terms for rowdy behavior, a loud noise, disturbance, or commotion. These things were originally called 'ruction' or 'rumpus'. Today, Ruckus has been gleefully reclaimed as a dynamic, gender-neutral baby name. It's also become common for pets and is even a clothing brand. If you consider rebellion a virtue, take this name.

S

S. Pellegrino
Saab
Saad
Sack
Sacrificial Lamb
Saddam
Saddie
Saddle Brown
Sadiska
Safety Orange
Safety Yellow
Saga
Saline
Saline Solution
Salman Rushdie
Salmon
Salomé
Salsa
Salty
Samsung
Samurai
San Andreas
San Serif
Sand Dune
Sandal
Sandwich

Saab

(saab)

Let's start with the name origin of 'Saab', the now historically significant, innovative automotive brand. It is actually a stylized acronym of sorts for 'Svenska Aeroplane Company'. Saab originated in 1937 as a national defense contractor. In 1945, they began making cars. Not any ordinary cars–very special cars: aerodynamic, often turbocharged, with a dual attention to safety and function. As imports, they tended to be driven by adventurous and quirky eccentrics, often obsessed with their own identity issues. Saab, the car company, sadly ceased operation in 2014. So, let your child become the next generation of Saab. We know he/she/them won't become just another 'Saab story'.

Sap
Sari
Satan
Sauce
Saucer
Sausage & Peppers
Salvage
Savage
Saved
Saw
'Say My Name'
'Say My Name Bitch'
Scabies
Scarface
Scarier
Scarlet Fever
Scary
Scenery
Scent
Scented
Schism
Schizo
Schlemiel
Schlep
Schllmazel
Schlub
Schmear
Schmeckel
Schmecker
Schmendrik
Schmo
Schmooze
Schmorlt
Schmutz
Schnook
School Bus
Schwarzenegger
Science Diet
Scientology
Scion
Scooby
Scooped
Scorch
SCOTUS
Scrapper
Scrapple
Scratch and Sniff
Scratchy
Scream
Screamer
Scrimmage
Scrod
Scroll
Scrub
Scrub Daddy
Scrubby Bubbles
SCUBA
Scythe

Scrimmage

(SKRI-muhj)

'Scrimmage'. What a great name for the scion of a sporting family. Forget about the name 'Rugby'—that's for dogs. Whether your baby is destined for soccer, football, or field hockey, Scrimmage will certainly make them stand out on their team roster.

Seabiscuit

Seal

Sealy

Sealy Dan

Second Law of Thermodynamics

Secrecy

Secretion

See Ya

SEED

Seed

Selfie

Senator

Senna

Señor

Sequel II

Serif

Sermon

SETI

Sex Pistol

Shade

Shadow

Shaft

Shafter

Shagg

Shallot

Sham

Shaman

Shampoo

Shamrock

Shangri-La

Shards

Shark

Sharkboy

Sharknada

Sharknado

Shart

Shattered

Shazam

She-Hulk

Sheesh

Sherpa

Shiksa

Ship Happens

Shitty-Ass

Shizzle

Shocker

Shocking Pink

Shoegaze

Shoofly

Shoofly Pie

Shook

Shooker

Shoosh

Short

Short Circuit

Shortie

Shortie Of

Shout

Serif

(SEH-ruhf)

Consider the serif. It is the underappreciated hero of typography. Yes, we can admire the slender grace and stylish presence of such modern fonts as Helvetica and Bauhaus, but if we really want to read, absorb, and appreciate good writing, we need the serif (ask any newspaperman). As a name, therefore, 'Serif' denotes a devotion to classicism, learning, and literary traditions. Without the serif, such qualities would be forever lost.

Siri

(SEE-ree)

At this point, 'Siri' may seem trite as a name for your daughter. Of course, it originally comes from Norwegian, meaning 'a beautiful woman who leads you into victory'. In recent years, we have come to know Siri as the calm and soothing voice of our iPhone. In fact, Siri's AI origins go back to a US government-funded project, CALO (Cognitive Assistant that Learns and Observes). Can your new baby grow to be your own 'cognitive assistant'? Through 'learning' and 'observation'? By now, poignantly, Siri's undeniable brilliance may have been eclipsed by ChatGPT. She is a new woman come along who seems to know *more*. And she certainly seems to know more about *you*. So, we ask you to consider Siri as a nostalgic name that harkens back to a golden age of innocence at the dawn of AI.

Shovel
Shrimp
Shrub
Shtit
Shuttlecock
Sibling
Sidebar
Siemens
Sigma
Simile
Simp
Simulator
Sin
Sinker
Siri
Sistah
Sister Sledge
Sith
67
Sizzle
Skarlit Feevur
Skee-Ball
Skibidi
Skipper
Skippy
Skittle
Skullbone
Skullcandy
Skullgirl
Slam Dunk
Slappy
Slatsy
Slavia
Slay
Slayer
Sleep
Sleepy
Slemmestad
Slice
Slick Willie
Slider
Slimfast
Slither
Slizké
Sloop
Sloth
Slug
Slugger
Sluggoth
Sluggy
Slumber
Slur
Slutsk
Smartie
Smear
Smirk
Smitten
Smokin'

Slizké

(sliz-KAY)

Looking for some Slavic flavoring or pride in your baby's name? Consider 'Slizké', after a sleek-sounding locale in Slovakia. It's a name that sounds like a noun and an adjective at the same time. It might only be the name of a small town, but that town has its own flag!

Smoky
Smoothie
Smort
Smurf
Smurfette
Smushy
Snake
Snap-On
Snapper
Snapple
Snark
Snarker
Snatch
Snausage
Snausage in a Blanket
Sneaker
Snicker
Snickers
Snitch
Snowman
Snuckie
Sodom
Soft Spread
Software
SONAR
Sorbet
Sorrow
Sorry
Sort Of
Soul Eater
Soulja Boy
Soulja Boy Baby Mother
Sour Patch Kid
SouthEast
South Sudan
Soylent Green
'Soylent Green is People!'
Spa
Space Cadet
Space X
Spaghetti
Spaghetti Western
Spam
Spanish Whore
Spanky
Spanx
Sparklefarts
Sparky
Spawn
Special K
SPECTRE
Speed
Speed Racer
Speedometer
Spermbanken
SPF
Sphere
Spic and Span

Spicy
Spiritbox
Splenda
Splinter
Splooge
Splunge
Spook
Spool
Spooner
Spore
Sportster
Spray
Spray-On
Spriggan
Spring Chicken
Sprite
Sputnik 1
Squadron
Squalor
Squarefoot
Squash
Squatty
Squeaky
Squeeze
Squeezer
Squick
Squid
Squirrel
Squirt
Squirter
Sri Lanka
Sssnake
St. Helens
St. Patrick
Stage Whisper
Stain
Stainz
Stalin
Stammer
Stapler
Starburst
Starfleet
Stash
Static
Stayin' Alive
Stealth
STEM
Stendra
Stephen Hawking
Stepmonster
Steppenwolf
Steroid
Stiff
Stigma
Stigmata
Stiletta
Stiletto
Stinger

Sorbet

(SOR-bay)

'Sorbet' immediately sounds sweet—and French (although potentially icy.) Sorbet conjures associations of high-end restaurants and glamorous sidewalk cafés. Just imagine you are at La Glace Alain Ducasse, near the Champs-Elysées, Paris. Here you are met with lemon, candied lemon, and grapefruit vermouth sorbet varieties. Your baby's name could also elicit such exotic, tasty associations.

Stitch
Stone Cold
Stoner
Stop
Storm
Storyboard
Straight
Stranger
Streisand
Strive
Stroker
Strong Lime
Strunz
Stubby
Stud
Studd
Student
Stuffed
Stuffy
Stumble
Stung
Stutter
Subaru
Subgenre
SubReddit
Suburb
Subwoofer
Successor
Sudafed
Suds
Sudski
Sudsy
Suedehead
Sufficiente
Sugarfoot
Sulfur
Summation
Sun Ra
Sun Ra Arkestra
Supah
Supra
Supreme
Surge
Surreal
Surrender
Surrogate
Survival
Survive
Survivor
Sus
Sushi
Suzuki
Svelte
Svenskehølet
Swag
Swagg
Swagger
Swaggy

Spanx

(spangks)

'Spanx'. Or may we suggest 'Spanxx'? Or even 'Spanxxx'? In the year 2000, innovative undergarment clothier Sara Blakely gamely launched her brand of footless, body-shaping wearables. At the time, some Middle American retailers considered the name risqué. However, they were soon won over by the tagline 'Don't worry, we've got your butt covered'. Okay, we know that you are not supposed to spank your child anymore. But that doesn't mean you can't Spanx him/her/them. For a more retro association, consider 'Spanky' from the *Our Gang/Little Rascals* vintage TV shows. In that case, if more siblings were to come along, you could call them 'Alfalfa', 'Buckwheat', 'Porky', or even the lesser-known 'Wheezer'.

Swale
Swallow
Swamp Thing
Swank
SWAT
Sweeney Todd
Sweet Tart
Swerve
Swifter
Swiftie
Swinger
Swipe
Switch
Switch Hitter
Swizz
Swole
Swoosh
Symbolic
Synonym
Syntax
Synthetic Opioid
Synthroid
System
Szparki

T

T. Fungus
T.K.O.
T.P.
Tabby
Taboo
Tabular
Taco
Tactile
Tailchaser
Taint
Talc
Tang
Tango
Tango & Cash
Tank
Tank Girl
Tank Grrl
Tantric
Tantrica
Tarantula
Target
Tariff
Tart
Tarzan
Tarzana
TASER
Taskmaster
Taste of the Wild

Tariff

(TEH-ruhf)

A noble name, 'Tariff' derives from the Arabic word *tarifa*, meaning 'notification' or 'information'. It has been used for centuries in the Ottoman Empire and Persia. You may have already considered the name 'Heathcliff'. But what about Tariff? In fact, if your new baby just happens to be an import, Tariff might fit the bill.

Tasty
Tater Tot
Tattletale
Tattoo
Taunt
Taupe
Taze
Teal
Tech
Technique
Ted
Teeth
Tempest
Temptation
Tenacity
Tendernob
Tenure
Terminator
Terminator 2
Terrific
Terse
Textual
Texture
The Abyss
The Bat
The Blob
The Changeling
The Chosen
The Darkside
The East Wing
The Gorilla
The Hobbit
The Hunchback of Notre Dame
The Hunger
The Iron Sheik
The Joker
The King
The L Word
The Last Man
The Last of Us
The Lost Boy
The Martian
The Matrix
The Mindy Project
The Nanny
The North Face
The Omen
The Patriot Act
The Penguin
The Pianist
The Problem
The Professor
The Raven
The Riddler
The Rock
The Sandman
The Situation
The Solution
The Thing

The Western Canon
The Wire
The X-Files
Them
Themselves
TheQuickBrownFoxJumpedOvertheLazyDog
Therapy
They
They Fly
Thickening
Thingie
Thingus
3rd Person
Third Person
Third Wheel
Thirsty
Thistle
Thomas Pynchon
Thong
Thor
Thorin
Thought
Thrasher
Thrawn
3M
Three's Company
Throg
Throggs Neck
Throggs Neck Bridge
Throwblanket
Thumper
Thunder
Tickle Me
Tiddlywink
Tide
Tight End
Tightsqueeze
TikTok
Times New Roman
Timothy Leary
Tinder
Tinker Bell
Tiny
Titicaca
Titanic
Titus Andronicus
Titos
Toast
Tobacco
Tojota
Token
Tom of Finland
Tomb Raider
Tombstone
Tonk

Three's Company

(threes KUM-puh-nee)

Sometimes, a third child can create a problem. Especially for the middle child, who may have already grown accustomed to being 'The Baby'. Such a conundrum. Let us suggest the name 'Three's Company' as a lighthearted way of addressing this delicate situation, while also acknowledging its attendant psychological stresses. Also, it will keep the grandparents happy, as they no doubt cherish dear memories of the sitcom of the same name.

Tostita & Tostito

(tow-STEE-tah and tow-STEE-tow)

Everyone knows and enjoys the Tostito as something loveable, a food that we often share as a family. In Spanish, or Mexican Spanish, the '-o' ending is masculine. But what if you take it one step further—and name your daughter 'Tostita'? Then you would really be changing the norms of gender identity. Just don't call her 'Tostiloca'.

Tonka
Tooth
Top Gun
Torch
Torment
Tornado
Torpedo
Torque
Tosh
Tostita
Tostito
Total Drama
Total Recall
Touch
Tourette
Towelette
Toxic
Trader Joe
Tragedy
Trailer
Trammp
Train Wreck
Tranq
Transplant
Trapezoid
Trapezoida
Trapezoids
Trapped
Tremor
Tremors
Triangle
Tribal
Tribble
Triffid
Trigger
Trilogy
Triscuit
Triscuit Thin
Trojan
Troll
Trolling
Tron
Trope
Tropicana
Truant
Trust Yourself
Tsunami
Tubular
Tumbleweed
Turbine
Turtle
Twatt
Tweeny
Tweet
Tweeter
Twilight
Twin
Twinkie

Twister

Twitch

Twitter

Twix

Two-Seater

2Shy

Twrch

Tyke

Typo

U

Uber
Uberous
Ubi
Ubicity
Ubiquitarianism
Udometer
UFOlogy
Uganda
Ugg
Ugli
Ughten
Uh Oh
Ukulele
Ulmaceous
Uloid
Ultimate
Ultimo
Ultimatum
Ultramarine
Ululate
Ulysses
Umber
Umbilical
Umbrage
Umlaut
Ummagumma

Ummagumma

(UH-mah-gum-ah)

The sad fact is, the only people remaining who know the glorious history of the name 'Ummagumma' are those that lived through the era of 1960s British psychedelic rock music. And those people are either your parents—or your grandparents. Yet these happy geezers could provide a trove of valuable lore and naming possibilities. Just think: 'Cream' or 'King Crimson'. We have skipped over those obvious choices to bring you a true underground classic, Ummagumma. That was the name of Pink Floyd's breakthrough album, released November 7, 1969. Its best-known song is 'A Saucerful of Secrets'. Let that describe your child.

Unctious
Unbleached
Unarmed
Uncle Ben's
Uncle Betty
Undercover
Undergarment
Underground
Underrated
Undertaker
Undertow
Undiagnosed
Undo
Uneeda
Uneedus
Unfurl
Ungodly
UNICEF
Unicorn
Unicycle
Uniform
Unisex
UNO
Unplugged
Unreal
Unseen
Unsportsmanlike
Unsupervised
Unto
Upbeat
Upchuck
Updo
Uppercut
Upside
Upsurge
UR
Ur
Uranium
Uranus
Urchin
Urge
Urgent
Urology
Ursa
Uruguay
US Agent
Used
Username
User-Friendly
User-Friendly Interface
Utz Girl
Uvula
Uzbeki
Uzi

Uncle Ben's

(UHNG-kuhl benz)

Yes, it's a direct possessive, but 'Uncle Ben's' is also fantastic and dependable stovetop rice!

Undertaker

(UHN-dr-tay-kr)

Lest we forget—morticians, funeral directors, and embalmers are the unsung heroes among us. These tireless, self-appointed public servants provide us solace during our most difficult times. And as anyone in small-town USA already knows, undertaking is a family business, proudly passed from generation to generation. (An undertaker often owns the nicest house in the neighborhood, usually a former mansion.) Today, the name 'Undertaker' has 'overtaken' our imaginations, as it has been co-opted in popular culture, first by a WWE professional wrestler of distinction, then by a monster truck.

V

Vader
Vagi
Vaginal
Val-Zod
Valkyrie
Valvoline
Vampair
Vampyre
Vandal
Vans
Vape
Varathane
Vargr
Vaseline
Vato
Vault
Vegemite
Velcro
Velveeta
Vengeance
Veni Vidi Vici
Venom
Ventolin Inhaler
Verb
Verbal
Vermouth

Valvoline

(VAL-vuh-leen)

A personal favorite of ours, a name with a distinct melodic cadence. Yes, 'Valvoline' is a classic American motor oil brand, dating back to 1873. Its reputation is that of 'The Original Lubricant'. Of course, we know Valvoline by its bold, stylish logo and long association with automobile racing. Consider your baby a possible 'social lubricant' into the new world of parenthood. 'Valvoline, sound thy name'.

Vermouth

(vr-MOOTH)

As a sophisticated aperitif, Vermouth's potent secret lies in its flavorful hint of *Artemesia absinthium*. Imagine a possible future courtship: 'Artemesia', meet 'Vermouth'. This Hippocratic wine dates back to ancient Greece. Now, we know it as an essential Martini ingredient. Which could be shaken, not stirred.

Verso
Vertigo
Viagra
Vibe
Victory Royale
Victim 1
Victim 2
Vile
Vine
Viper
Virgin
Virus
Visa
Viscera
Visine
Visitor
Vitamin
Viva Las Vegas
Vivid
Vlad
Vodka
Volumina
Voluminous
Volumizer
Volunteer
Volvic
Voodoo
Vroom
Vroom Vroomer
Vroomer
Vulcan

W

Waffle

Wag

Waggy

Walking Dead

Wallop

Walrus

Wank

Warhammer

Warhead

Warhol

Wasabi

Washable

Washer

Wasp

Watafak?

Watco

Watergate

Waterloo

Watermelon

Waterproof

Weapon

Weather

Weener

Weezer

Weezy

Werewolf

Watergate & Waterloo

(WAA-tr-gayt and waw-ter-LOO)

The choice is yours: 'Watergate' or 'Waterloo'. Both names carry weighty historical distinction. The architecturally distinctive Watergate Hotel in Washington, DC, became known for its link to the scandal that brought down President Richard Nixon in the 1970s. Waterloo, similarly, caused the downfall of the most notorious European emperor, Napoleon, in *the Battle of Waterloo* of 1815. Both names are still undeniably powerful and resonant, even today.

Wetwang
Whack-a-Mole
Wham!
Whatever
Whipped Vanilla
Whippet
Whiskas
White Musk
White Rice
Whitewash
Whoopi
Why
Wicket
Widow
Widowmaker
Wienermobile
wifi
Wiki
Wild Thing
Wild Thang
Willard
William S. Burroughs
Willing
Willpower
Windex
WingDing
Wingman
Winnebago
Winx
Wisdom
Wisdom Tooth
Withered
Woke
Wolfman
Wolverine
Wonka
Woo
Woody
Woof
Woofer
Word Salad
Worf
Workbench
Worm
Worms
Wraith
Wreck
Wrinkle

X

X

x-Factor

X:

Xaar

Xanadu

Xanax

Xanthic

Xawa

Xbox

X-Chromosome (better for girls)

Xenon

Xerox

Xi

XL

Xocolatlite

Xolair

XOXO

xtra

XXL

XXX

Xxxxxxzzzlp

Xysma

Xenon

(ZEE-naan)

'Xenon' is a baby name with futuristic verve. A rare noble gas, Xenon's discovery came alongside 'Krypton' and 'Neon'. Together, they're like *The Three Amigos* of noble gases. (Xenon, by far, has the sexiest name of the three.) It's such a great name that was taken by a leading discotheque in 1970s New York City, known for clientele like Andy Warhol and Mick Jagger. Xenon catered to an upwardly mobile crowd. Let your child become one of them. Or let your child become *the* one of them.

XOXO

(EKS-oh-EKS-oh or zoh-zoh)

'XOXO', we know, means 'hugs and kisses'. This is all a baby really needs. Pronounced aloud, XOXO has an exotic sound, almost Russian in its intonation.

Y

Y'all

Y3

Ya Ya

Yachty

Yahoo!

Yahtzee

Yak

Yam Yam

Yanni

Yardarm

Yardstick

Yarn

Yastrzemski

Yawny

Y-Chromosome (better for boys)

Yearling

Yearly

Yearn

Yeasty

Yeezus

Yeezy

Yeezy Pods

Yeezy Slides

Yegg

Yellow Crayon

Yellow-Bellied Weasel

Yellowbelly

Yahtzee

(YAH-tsee)

No one knows the identity of the mysterious Canadian couple said to have first inspired this unique dice game by playing it on their yacht. Now 'Yahtzee' has come to be associated with both skill *and* chance. So, go ahead, roll the dice and choose Yahtzee. If you at first don't score, roll again. You just might end up with a full house! But beware: There is a joker rule.

Yanni

(YAA-nee)

'Yanni', a popular Greek name meaning 'God is gracious', comes from the Greek Orthodox. In Hebrew, it is 'Yochanan'. The name has become synonymous with the global musical superstar Yanni (Yiannis Chryssomallis). Yanni is known for his fusion of classical, soft-rock, and world music—all set to lush orchestral accompaniment. So considered for your baby, a golden metaphorical association indeed.

Yelp
Yemen
Yenta
Yes
Yeti
Yikes!
Yin
Yippee!
Yoda
Yoda Plushie
Yodel
Yoga
Yogurt
Yohji Yamamoto
Yoicks!
Yoke
Yolk
YOLO
Yonkers
Yoplait
Young Fabulous & Broke
Your Image Here
Your Logo Here
Your Mum
YourFaceMyArse
YouTube
Yowie!
Yowza
Yoyo
Yttrium
Yu Gothic
Yucatan
Yucca
Yuengling
Yugo
Yule Log
Yummy
Yurt
Yves Saint Laurent

Your Mum

(yor mum)

'Your Mum'. Truly, what a loving tribute to the one who does it all! And the one who made it all happen! We can thank the Brits for this one.

Z

Zaddy
Zanazzite
Zap
Zapfino
Zaphnathpaaneah
Zarathustra
Zarqa
Zed
Zeitgeist
Zero
Zero Hour
Zest
Zilla
Zimbabwe
Zincobotryogen
Zinnwaldite
Zinzolin
Ziploc
Zippy
Ziti
Zoloft
Zombie
Zomp
Zoom
Zygote
Zyklon
Zyns
Zyrtec
ZZZ
Zzzzzzz Mm Rrrr Pppqqq Zzz

Ziti

(ZEE-tee)

Perhaps we have not yet taken ample opportunity to delve into the delectable and flavorsome potential of food names. Some that have already been adopted by progressive parents include: 'Anis', 'Basil', 'Cinnamon', 'Clementine', 'Ginger', and 'Kale'. Not to mention the old classic, 'Peaches'. What about 'Ziti'? Italian cuisine is best known for its emphasis on tradition and family. 'Buono', 'Delizioso', 'Squisito', 'Fresco'! And pasta is the greatest comfort food of them all. With names that carry zest and attitude: 'Farfalle', 'Penne', 'Gnocchi'. Such names often end with an 'i' or an 'e', but they may be modified with an 'a' ending to become feminine.

ZZZ

(buzzing zee)

'ZZZ'. Goodnight, Dear Baby.

APPENDIX

Top 10 Terrible Baby Names from the 1950s

1. Sputnik 1
2. Ike
3. Krushchev
4. Maybellene
5. Johnny B. Goode
6. Juke
7. Howl
8. Ankle Biter
9. Pez
10. Edsel

Top 10 Terrible Baby Names from the 1960s

1. Jimi
2. Janis
3. Jim
4. Barbie
5. Beehive
6. Perm
7. Afro
8. Twiggy
9. Snoopy
10. Square

Top 10 Terrible Baby Names from the 1970s

1. Farrah
2. Cher
3. Rubik
4. Weeble
5. Taxi
6. Taxi Driver
7. Mork
8. Mindy
9. Kojak
10. Jaws

Top 10 Terrible Baby Names from the 1980s

1. Pac Man
2. J.R.
3. E.T.
4. Terminator
5. Dune
6. Whopper
7. Byte
8. Lite
9. Celica
10. DeLorean

Top 10 Terrible Baby Names from the 1990s

1. Moby
2. Bjork
3. Tupac
4. Fugee
5. Jurassic
6. Blockbuster
7. Target
8. Game Boy
9. Tamagotchi
10. Hummer

Top 10 Terrible Baby Names Based on Disco Songs

1. Boogie
2. Hot Stuff
3. Sister Sledge
4. Trammp
5. Le Freak
6. Love Thang
7. Lipps Inc.
8. Night Fever
9. Car Wash
10. Stayin' Alive

Top 10 Terrible Baby Names for New Englanders

1. Pilgrim
2. Puritan
3. Radcliffe
4. Foliage
5. Lobster
6. Scrod
7. Packie
8. Yastrzemski
9. Nor’easter
10. Rizdee

Top 10 Terrible Baby Names for Texans

1. Howdy
2. Y'All
3. Chili
4. Spurs
5. Burr
6. Alamo
7. Longhorn
8. Skeeter
9. Tarnation
10. Chimichanga

Top 10 Terrible Baby Names for Midwesterners

1. Buckeye
2. Cheesehead
3. Piston
4. Packer
5. Chief
6. Soil
7. Soybean
8. Euchre
9. Schlitz
10. Blatz

Top 10 Terrible Baby Names for the Pacific Northwest

1. Grunge
2. Bigfoot
3. Log
4. Halibut
5. Boeing
6. Totem
7. Starbucks
8. Kayak
9. Hydroelectric
10. Snowpocalypse

Top 10 Terrible Baby Names for Californians

1. Artichoke
2. Dude
3. Gnarly
4. Flea
5. Kush
6. Vape
7. Getty
8. Altamont
9. Gidget
10. In-N-Out

Top 10 Terrible Baby Names That Sound Canadian

1. Eh
2. Hoser
3. Keener
4. Beaver
5. Oiler
6. 'Jesus Murphy'
7. 'Torono'
8. Ottawa
9. Snowbird
10. Zed

Top 10 Terrible Baby Names That Could Be Mistaken for Food

1. Hammy
2. Egbert
3. Caesar
4. Bree
5. Reuben
6. Pepper
7. Roux
8. Madeleine
9. Chip
10. Alaska

Top 10 Terrible Baby Names That Sound like Weapons

1. Uzi
2. Rocket
3. Rock
4. Paper
5. Scissors
6. Glock
7. Trigger
8. Mace
9. Gunner
10. Howitzer

Top 10 Terrible Baby Names That Would Be Great in the Witness Protection Program

1. Lucky
2. Secret
3. Gone
4. Ammon
5. Gudrun
6. Harlem
7. Chameleon
8. Vamoose
9. Cloak
10. Guilty

Top 10 Terrible Baby Names That Sound like Pharmaceutical Drugs

1. Zenobia
2. Anastasia
3. Lavinia
4. Malia
5. Gaia
6. Ophelia
7. Saskia
8. Zosia
9. Zinnia
10. Xenia

Top 10 Terrible Baby Names That Would Make Great Pet Names

1. Rex
2. Maisy
3. Duke
4. Billy
5. Scout
6. Hercules
7. Jasper
8. Luna
9. Milo
10. Dino

Top 10 Terrible Baby Names Derived from the Writings of Immanuel Kant

1. To Be
2. Admiration
3. Awe
4. Dignity
5. Critique
6. Reason
7. Universal
8. Enlightenment
9. Will
10. Maxim

Top 10 Terrible Baby Names from Sports

1. GOAT
2. FIFA
3. Baller
4. Banjax
5. Dribble
6. Fumble
7. Curveball
8. Punch
9. Punt
10. Switch Hitter

About the Authors

Jack and John Zinsser
Photo by Charlotte Zinsser

John Zinsser is a noted abstract painter who has done over 40 solo exhibitions in the US and Europe. He is also a writer on contemporary art and has been a longtime instructor at The New School University in New York City. In 1992, his treatise, *750 Standard Painting Titles*, was published by Elizabeth Koury Gallery and soon became a cult item.

Jack Zinsser, John Zinsser's son, is a junior publishing executive at The Stable Book Group. John and Jack are the son and grandson, respectively, of the late beloved author William Zinsser (*On Writing Well*).